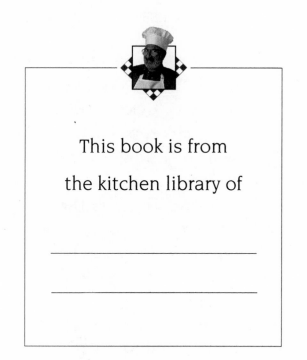

This book is from

the kitchen library of

_____

_____

ALSO BY ART GINSBURG, MR. FOOD®

The Mr. Food® Cookbook, OOH IT'S SO GOOD!!™ (1990)

Mr. Food® Cooks Like Mama (1992)

Mr. Food® Cooks Chicken (1993)

Mr. Food® Cooks Pasta (1993)

Mr. Food® Makes Dessert (1993)

Mr. Food® Cooks Real American (1994)

Mr. Food®'s Favorite Cookies (1994)

Mr. Food®'s Quick and Easy Side Dishes (1995)

Mr. Food® Grills It All in a Snap (1995)

Mr. Food®'s Fun Kitchen Tips and Shortcuts (and Recipes, Too!) (1995)

Mr. Food®'s Old World Cooking Made Easy (1995)

"Help, Mr. Food®! Company's Coming!" (1995)

Mr. Food® Pizza 1-2-3 (1996)

Mr. Food® Meat Around the Table (1996)

Mr. Food® Simply Chocolate (1996)

Mr. Food® A Little Lighter (1996)

Mr. Food® From My Kitchen to Yours: Stories and Recipes from Home (1996)

Mr. Food® Easy Tex-Mex (1997)

Mr. Food® One Pot, One Meal (1997)

Mr. Food® COOL CRAVINGS

Easy Chilled and Frozen Desserts

Art Ginsburg

Mr. Food®

WILLIAM MORROW AND COMPANY, INC.

NEW YORK

Library of Congress Cataloging-in-Publication Data

Ginsburg, Art.
    Mr. Food® cool cravings / Art Ginsburg.
       p.   cm.
    Includes index.
    ISBN 0-688-14579-5
    1. Desserts.   2. Frozen desserts.   I. Title.
TX773.G486   1997
641.8'6—dc21   97-9547
                             CIP

Printed in the United States of America

First Edition

1 2 3 4 5 6 7 8 9 10

BOOK DESIGN BY MICHAEL MENDELSOHN OF MM DESIGN 2000, INC.

Dedicated to
The "tastiest treats" of all—
my new granddaughters,

Alyssa Renée and Noa Michelle

Contents

Acknowledgments

Many parts have to *gel* in order to write a good cookbook. And, thanks to my outstanding team, I think we've got another winner. When I told my staff we were going to create a cookbook filled with refrigerated and frozen desserts, they thought I was *"pudding"* them on . . . but I wasn't!

Step into my cooler and meet the wonderful folks who made this book happen: Patty, Janice, Cheryl, Joan, and Karen *buttered me up* with all the recipes we tested and retested to cool perfection. Joe, Laura, and Helayne planned and documented our work in the kitchen with their usual *crisp* attention to detail. Al kept us *rolling* along smoothly, and Steve, Chuck, Ethel, Tom, Chet, Marilyn, Beth, Alice, and Carol *egged us on* as they gladly tasted our creations. Thanks a bunch—you guys are the COOLEST!

My creative partners, Howard and Caryl, have brought everything together once again to satisfy your *craving* for another Mr. Food cookbook full of yummy recipes and kitchen fun. As always, these guys make it all as *easy as pie*!

My friends at William Morrow—Al, Paul, Zach, Lisa, Deborah, Anne, Michael, Jackie, and Richard—are, without a doubt, the *cream of the crop*. A great big thanks to all of you and to my agent, Bill, my designer, Michael, and my illustrator, Philip—my *rock solid* supporters.

And you, my friends, are the *icing on the cake*! Thanks for making it possible for me to keep bringing you a great big helping of *"OOH IT'S SO GOOD!!®"*

Introduction

How many times have the kids come home from school, opened the refrigerator, and just stood there looking for something to jump out at them and say, "Here I am! I'm what you feel like eating!" And how 'bout all those times when, after about an hour or so of sitting in front of the TV, you go to the freezer to see what's in there that can satisfy your desire for something cool and sweet?

Well, if we talked to scientists who study people's eating habits, we'd probably get a long explanation for why we feel the need for cool, refreshing sweets. But I learned a lot while putting together this book, and I'd rather forget about scientific reasons and call it simply a case of the "Cool Cravings"!

I guess you're not surprised to find out that a lot of us share this "gotta have something sweet *now*!" feeling. That's why I want you to have these prescriptions . . . I mean recipes . . . that are guaranteed to do the trick!

In my fruit chapter, you'll find remedies for satisfying some of your simplest cool cravings. Look for everything from Spirited Fruit Cocktail (page 39) to compote, ambrosia, and even Chocolate-Laced Fruit Kebabs (page 44).

For something else that's light and refreshing, why not try some pudding or gelatin—or maybe a trifle or parfait? With recipes such as Tropical Gelatin Salad (page 29), Caramel Vanilla Pudding Surprise (page 21), Strawberry Kiwi Trifle (page 4), and Cherry Cola Parfaits (page 8), these chapters are full of cooling winners.

But if those aren't the answer, it's time to turn to the chapter of chilled cakes. There's everything from All-American Strawberry

Introduction

Shortcake (page 64) to classic and tasty Cassata Cake (page 54) and Coconut Dream Cake (page 65). With just one bite, you'll know exactly how *that* one got its name!

Okay, so you're in desperate need of something *really* cool, *really* rich, and *really* impossible to resist . . . so it's time to explore a chapter brimming with cheesecakes! I'm talking about real cheesecakes—*big* cheesecakes—and, boy, what an assortment of flavors I've got for you. Your cheesecake craving can lead you to one of my favorites, White Chocolate Macadamia Cheesecake (page 71). Or maybe German Black Bottom Cheesecake (page 72) is what you feel like having. It doesn't matter which one you choose, 'cause you're in for a treat with any of these!

Then again, maybe you'd like to cool down with a refreshing piece of refrigerated pie. Have I got some super ones in here . . . and, yes, they're all easy as you-know-what to make. Maybe your taste buds are anxious for the light taste of Fresh Strawberry Pie (page 91)? Or are they searching for something more sinful like Cappuccino Custard Pie (page 90) or Pecan-Crusted Chocolate Pie (page 101)? Wow! And that's only the beginning!

If you're leaning more toward frozen treats, we've got those, too! The frozen dessert chapter is loaded with choices for block-busters like Block Party Ice Cream Cake (page 107) and Chocolate Chip Dome (page 121). That one looks so darned complicated, yet it's simply layer after layer of just four ingredients.

And we can always count on the freezer as the place to go for a bit of novelty. That's right . . . we can make a whole collection of fun frozen treats like Chocolate Pudding Pops (page 127) and Drop-in Ice Cream Sandwiches (page 130) that are perfect quick snacks for company, the kids, or us when we're on the go. We can stuff donuts with ice cream (page 138) and enjoy Chocolate-Cherry-Surprise Cupcakes (page 139) as easy as 1–2–3. Now, I can't tell you what *those* are packed with . . . you'll have to find out for yourself!

Introduction

If none of these recipes has been enough to satisfy your cool craving, get out the ice cream scoop and sundae dishes, 'cause there are incredible sorbets, ice creams, and other goodies in my chapter of Scoopable Delights. Now don't worry—you won't need an ice cream machine or loads of toppings for these yummies. Uh-uh! You can whip up your own homemade sauces and even Real Whipped Cream Dollops (page 172), to keep on hand for topping desserts as well as specialty coffees and other hot drinks in a matter of minutes.

Maybe you've been waiting for cool creations like Chocolate Napoleons (page 155) that even Napoleon would reach for with both hands! Or are you planning to fill a candy tray with goodies like Cranberry Clusters (page 163) and Almond Toffee Bars (page 166)? We've got 'em!

Why not promise to make your gang a different chilled dessert every month? Start the new year off right with Champagne Dessert Cocktails (page 183), celebrate the holidays with timely treats as the year progresses, and end it with No-Bake Holiday Fruitcake (page 200), which I promise is a lot easier (plus a whole lot tastier) than traditional fruitcake!

What are you waiting for?! It's time to get those cravings under control. And to keep them that way, keep this cookbook within easy reach. It's the best way to turn those "Cool Cravings" into loads of "OOH IT'S SO GOOD!!®"

Whip It Up

Wow! A whole book of refrigerated and frozen desserts! And lots of the recipes call for whipped cream or whipped topping. Yes, I often give you the option of using fresh whipped cream or prepared whipped topping. So let me give you a few pointers on each. (Refrigerated whipped cream that comes in aerosol-type cans is great for adding quick pizzazz to finished goodies, but it shouldn't be used in these recipes where fresh or frozen whipped cream or topping is indicated.)

To make fresh whipped cream, with an electric beater on high speed, whip heavy cream until stiff peaks form.

Tips:
1. Always keep the heavy cream cold until ready to whip. And, for best results, chill the bowl and beaters, too.
2. If you'd like to make flavored whipped cream, beat the cream until soft peaks form, then add a flavoring, extract, or liqueur and continue beating until stiff peaks form.
3. Do not overbeat cream. Doing so will make it curdle, eventually turning it into butter!
4. Avoid whipping cream in humid weather, as the cream will not whip well.
5. Whip cream as close as possible to serving time. If you must do it in advance, cover it tightly and store in the refrigerator until ready to use.

Today's supermarket freezer cases are loaded with whipped toppings. They're good substitutes for whipped cream and are available in many varieties, including traditional, low-fat, fat-free, and even flavored.

Frozen whipped topping needs to be thawed before using, and

it's best to do so overnight in the refrigerator. Do not microwave it or place the container in hot water to thaw.

Thawed whipped topping keeps for a couple of weeks in the refrigerator; that way it's always ready when we need it!

Wrap It Up

We can make the best-tasting desserts, but if they're not wrapped and stored properly, all the good taste can be overtaken by a stale taste from our refrigerator or freezer . . . not to mention the fact that our frozen goodies can become freezer-burned! Yuck!

So make certain to follow these few basic steps to keep each dessert packed with fresh-tasting flavor:

1. It's a good idea to start by placing toothpicks in the dessert and covering it loosely with plastic wrap just until chilled or frozen. This should keep the plastic wrap from attaching itself to icing or sticky edges.
2. After the dessert is chilled or frozen, it should be wrapped tightly with additional plastic wrap or aluminum foil. Better yet, there are lots of food storage containers available today that are perfect for the refrigerator and freezer.
3. Don't store your Cool Cravings near odor-producing foods such as onions and smoked meats. If you must, be sure each item is very well wrapped!
4. Always label food after wrapping, 'cause when the cool cravings hit, you won't want to be searching to see what's inside all the wrappers! Simply writing on a piece of masking tape with a waterproof marker works well.
5. It's a good idea to remove wrappers before thawing so they don't stick to the desserts.

6. Don't store desserts in the fridge or freezer for too long. The shelf life of desserts will vary, so use your common sense. One week in the fridge and thirty days in the freezer is usually the limit.
7. To keep your fridge and freezer fresh-smelling, use a box of baking soda or, even better, one of the new natural odor-absorbing products. They work well to get rid of unpleasant odors and extend the life of our favorite foods.

A Note About Packaged Foods

Packaged food sizes may vary by brand. Generally, the sizes indicated in these recipes are average sizes. If you can't find the exact package size listed in the ingredients, whatever package is closest in size will usually do the trick.

Trifles and Parfaits

The Sunshine Bowl

6 to 8 servings

During football season, we hear about all kinds of bowls. Well, I've got an edible bowl that you can serve anytime of the year to score really big with the gang!

2 packages (4 servings each) orange-flavored gelatin
1½ cups boiling water
1 cup cold water
1½ cups ice cubes
1 can (11 ounces) mandarin orange sections, drained
1 can (8 ounces) pineapple chunks, drained and juice reserved
1 pound cake (10¾ ounces), cut into 1-inch cubes
1½ cups cold milk
1 package (4-serving size) instant vanilla pudding and pie filling
¾ cup frozen whipped topping, thawed, divided

In a large bowl, dissolve the gelatin in the boiling water. Add the cold water and ice cubes, stirring until slightly thickened. Stir in the orange sections and pineapple chunks, reserving 4 pieces of each for garnish. Place the cake cubes in a trifle dish or large glass serving bowl and pour the reserved pineapple juice over the top. Spoon the gelatin mixture over the cake, then chill for 20 minutes. Meanwhile, in a large bowl, combine the milk and pudding mix, mixing thoroughly for 1 to 2 minutes, or until well blended. Let stand for a few minutes to thicken, then gently fold in ½ cup whipped topping. Spoon over the gelatin mixture and chill for 3 to 4 hours. Garnish with the remaining ¼ cup whipped topping and the reserved orange and pineapple pieces. Serve, or cover and keep chilled until ready to serve.

NOTE: Any leftover yellow or white cake (with or without icing) will work in place of the pound cake.

3

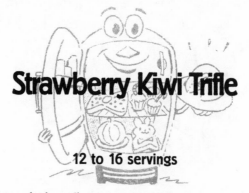

Strawberry Kiwi Trifle

12 to 16 servings

Who ever said English trifles weren't exciting?

1 can (14 ounces) sweetened
　　condensed milk
1 cup cold water
1 package (4-serving size) instant
　　vanilla pudding and pie filling
2 cups frozen whipped topping,
　　thawed

1 chocolate pound cake (16 ounces),
　　cut into 1-inch cubes
⅓ cup orange juice
1 quart fresh strawberries, sliced
2 kiwifruit, peeled and sliced

In a large bowl, combine the sweetened condensed milk and water; stir until well blended. Add the pudding mix and beat with an electric beater on low speed for 1 minute. Stir in the whipped topping until well blended. Place half the cake cubes in a trifle dish or large glass serving bowl. Drizzle half the orange juice over the cake. Cover with half the pudding mixture, then top with half the strawberries and kiwis. Repeat the layers, cover, and chill for at least 2 hours, or until ready to serve.

Cranberry Orange Trifle

12 to 14 servings

There's only one word for this dessert . . . scrumptious! And you'll be hearing that each and every time you serve it.

1 can (16 ounces) whole berry cranberry sauce
1 container (16 ounces) frozen whipped topping, thawed

5 medium-sized oranges, peeled and sectioned
1 pound cake (16 ounces), cut into 16 slices

In a large bowl, combine the cranberry sauce and whipped topping until thoroughly mixed. In a trifle dish or large glass serving bowl, layer one quarter of the orange sections, 4 slices of pound cake, and one quarter of the cranberry mixture. Repeat the layers 3 more times, ending with the cranberry mixture. Cover and chill for at least 1 hour, or until ready to serve.

NOTE: If you prefer, you can slice the oranges instead of sectioning them, then use them to line the sides of the trifle dish for a pretty presentation.

Coconut Pecan Parfaits

6 to 8 servings

Appearances do count, 'cause even the simplest of desserts looks dressed up in the right serving dish.

1 cup flaked coconut, toasted (see Note)

1 package (6-serving size) instant vanilla pudding and pie filling, prepared according to the package directions

1 cup pecan pieces, toasted (see Note)

In a large bowl, combine the toasted coconut and the pudding; mix well. Spoon half the mixture evenly into 6 to 8 parfait glasses. Sprinkle half the pecans evenly over the pudding, then repeat the layers. Cover loosely and chill for at least 2 hours, or until ready to serve.

NOTE: To toast the coconut and nuts, spread them separately in a single layer on a large rimmed baking sheet and bake at 425°F. for 7 to 9 minutes, or until golden, stirring halfway through the toasting. (Keep an eye on them, because they may be ready sooner—and keeping them in the oven for too long will get you overdone or burned coconut and nuts!) Allow to cool completely before using.

Chocolate Almond Pudding

4 to 6 servings

Here's a pudding with the taste that's so popular in candy bars . . .
but it's much creamier and more satisfying *this* way.

⅔ cup sugar
¼ cup unsweetened cocoa
3 tablespoons cornstarch
¼ teaspoon salt
2¼ cups milk

½ teaspoon almond extract
   (see Note)
2 cups frozen whipped topping,
   thawed
1 cup sliced almonds, toasted

In a medium-sized saucepan, combine the sugar, cocoa, corn-starch, and salt. Gradually stir in the milk and bring to a boil over medium heat, stirring constantly. Remove from the heat and stir in the almond extract. Spoon into a large bowl and chill for at least 1 hour, or until completely cooled. Spoon half of the pudding evenly into 4 to 6 parfait glasses. Cover the pudding with half the whipped topping, then sprinkle with half the toasted almonds. Repeat the layers, then cover loosely and chill until ready to serve.

NOTE: Amaretto can be substituted for the almond extract, but without either, you've got great traditional homemade chocolate pudding.

Cherry Cola Parfaits

6 to 8 servings

The best way to serve these is in old-fashioned ice cream soda glasses. Everyone will do a double take when they see what's really inside!

2 packages (4 servings each) cherry-flavored gelatin
1⅔ cups boiling water
2 cups cola
1 cup chopped walnuts

1 cup chopped maraschino cherries
⅓ cup frozen whipped topping, thawed
3 plastic drinking straws, each cut in half

In a large bowl, dissolve the gelatin in the boiling water. Stir in the cola and chill for about 45 minutes. Stir in the chopped walnuts and cherries. Divide the mixture among 6 to 8 parfait glasses; cover and chill for 2 to 3 hours, or until set. When ready to serve, top each with a dollop of whipped topping. Serve garnished with the straws (just for fun).

NOTE: For even more cherry flavor, use cherry cola in place of regular cola. And, yup, you guessed it—it's okay to use either diet or caffeine-free cola, too.

8

Candy Apple Parfaits

4 to 6 servings

The taste of autumn mixed with the zip of cinnamon . . . without the sticks!

1¾ cups apple juice, divided
⅓ cup red-hot cinnamon candies
½ teaspoon vanilla extract
¼ teaspoon red food color
4 tart cooking apples, peeled, cored,
    and thinly sliced

3 tablespoons cornstarch
¾ cup graham cracker crumbs
¼ cup sugar
¼ cup (½ stick) butter, melted

In a large saucepan, combine 1½ cups apple juice, the cinnamon candies, vanilla, and food color; bring to a boil over medium heat, stirring constantly until the candies dissolve. Add the apples and return to a boil, stirring constantly. Reduce the heat to low and simmer for 10 to 12 minutes, or until the apples are tender, stirring frequently. In a small bowl, combine the remaining ¼ cup apple juice and the cornstarch; add to the apple mixture and stir for 1 to 2 minutes, or until thickened. Remove from the heat and set aside. In a medium-sized bowl, combine the graham cracker crumbs, sugar, and butter; mix well. Spoon one third of the apple mixture evenly into 4 to 6 parfait glasses. Sprinkle one third of the crumb mixture over the apples. Repeat the layers 2 more times. Chill for about 2 hours and serve, or cover and keep chilled until ready to serve.

NOTE: These look great topped with a dollop of whipped cream and some additional cinnamon candies.

9

Old-time Diner Gelatin Parfaits

8 servings

Remember how we all enjoyed the comfort of the blue plate special at the diner? And remember how no matter how full we were, there was always room for dessert? Well, here's why!

1 package (4-serving size) cherry-flavored gelatin, mixed according to the package directions
1 package (4-serving size) lime-flavored gelatin
1 cup boiling water
1½ cups ice cubes, divided

½ cup sour cream
1 can (8 ounces) pineapple tidbits, drained
1 can (5.5 ounces) apricot nectar
1 package (4-serving size) orange- or peach-flavored gelatin

Pour the cherry gelatin evenly into 8 large parfait glasses. Chill for 2 hours, or until set. In a large bowl, dissolve the lime gelatin in the boiling water. Add ½ cup ice cubes and mix until the cubes are melted and the gelatin is slightly thickened. With an electric beater on low speed, beat in the sour cream. Fold in the pineapple tidbits and layer evenly over the cherry gelatin. Chill for 2 hours, or until set. In a small saucepan, bring the apricot nectar to a boil over medium-high heat. In a medium-sized bowl, dissolve the orange or peach gelatin in the boiling apricot nectar. Add the remaining 1 cup ice cubes and stir until melted. Spoon over the lime gelatin layer in each parfait glass, then cover and chill for at least 3 hours, or until set.

NOTE: For a fruit-packed parfait, add a can of drained canned apricot halves to the final layer.

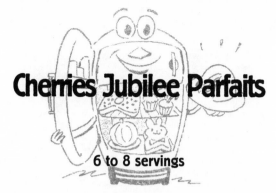

Cherries Jubilee Parfaits

6 to 8 servings

In fancy restaurants, cherries jubilee is often served flaming. This one's served ice-cold. It's got the same big taste, but with a much smaller price tag!

1½ cups cold milk
1 package (4-serving size) instant vanilla pudding and pie filling
1 cup frozen whipped topping, thawed

2 tablespoons sliced almonds, toasted, divided
1 can (20 ounces) light cherry pie filling

In a medium-sized bowl, combine the milk and pudding mix and whisk until slightly thickened. Gently stir in the whipped topping and 1 tablespoon almonds. Layer half the pudding mixture and half the cherry pie filling evenly into 6 to 8 parfait glasses. Repeat the layers and garnish with the remaining almonds. Cover loosely and chill for at least 2 hours before serving.

NOTE: If you want, add some additional whipped topping before garnishing with the almonds.

Puddings and Gelatins

13

Butterscotch Pudding

4 to 6 servings

Forget the "same old, same old" and tempt those taste buds with a new (really an old) flavor for a change. They'll love it—and the proof will be in the pudding *bowl* . . . 'cause it'll be empty!

½ cup firmly packed dark brown
    sugar
½ cup (1 stick) butter
¼ teaspoon salt

¼ cup cornstarch
2½ cups milk
2 teaspoons vanilla extract

In a medium-sized saucepan, combine the brown sugar, butter, and salt over medium heat. Cook for 3 to 4 minutes, or until the butter melts and the sugar begins to caramelize, stirring constantly; remove from the heat. In a medium-sized bowl, combine the cornstarch and milk, then whisk into the brown sugar mixture. Cook over medium heat for 5 to 6 minutes, or until the mixture has thickened, whisking constantly. Remove from the heat. Whisk in the vanilla and pour into a serving bowl or individual serving dishes. Chill for at least 2 hours; serve, or cover and keep chilled until ready to serve.

NOTE: For extra crunch, I like to serve this topped with some chopped-up chocolate-covered toffee candy bars. Of course, you should use *your* favorites.

Banana Pudding

4 servings

No boxed pudding here—just fresh-tasting big banana flavor. They'll go ape over it!

¼ cup sugar
2 tablespoons cornstarch
⅛ teaspoon salt
1 medium-sized ripe banana, mashed

2 egg yolks, beaten
½ teaspoon vanilla extract
1½ cups milk

In a small saucepan, combine the sugar, cornstarch, and salt. Add the banana, egg yolks, and vanilla, then place over medium-low heat and slowly whisk in the milk until thoroughly combined. Cook for 3 to 5 minutes, or until the mixture comes to a boil and thickens, whisking continuously. Spoon into a serving bowl or individual dessert dishes and chill thoroughly; serve, or cover and keep chilled until ready to serve.

NOTE: For an extra-special banana-chocolate treat, mix in ½ cup (3 ounces) miniature chocolate chips after the pudding has cooled slightly.

S'more Pudding

9 servings

Anybody who's gone to camp should remember roasting those yummy s'mores around the campfire. They'd just melt in your mouth. . . . Well, with just a few changes, we can relive those campfire flavors right at home.

11 whole graham crackers
1 package (4-serving size) cook-and-
serve chocolate pudding and pie
filling, prepared according to the
package directions and still hot

3 cups miniature marshmallows

Preheat the broiler. Place 4½ graham crackers in a single layer on the bottom of an 8-inch square metal baking pan. Spoon half the hot pudding over the graham crackers. Top with 1½ cups marshmallows, then another layer of 4½ graham crackers, pressing down gently. Spoon the remaining pudding on top, then sprinkle with the remaining 1½ cups marshmallows. Place under the broiler for 2 to 3 minutes, or until the marshmallows are golden and begin to melt. Crush the remaining 2 graham crackers and sprinkle over the melted marshmallows. Allow to cool, then cover and chill overnight to allow the graham crackers to soften. Cut into squares and serve.

NOTE: Maybe you'd like to lighten this up a bit? Use reduced-fat graham crackers and low-fat milk.

17

Chocolate Drizzle Bread Pudding

9 to 12 servings

Now, this is my idea of leftovers! Yes, yesterday's bread makes a great base for today's fresh dessert.

2½ cups milk
3 eggs
½ cup sugar
1 teaspoon vanilla extract

1 loaf (1 pound) Italian bread, cut into 1-inch cubes
1 cup (6 ounces) semisweet chocolate chips, melted

Preheat the oven to 325°F. In a large bowl, whisk together the milk, eggs, sugar, and vanilla. Add the bread cubes and toss gently, then let stand for about 15 minutes, or until the liquid is absorbed. Place half the bread mixture in a 7" × 11" baking dish that has been coated with nonstick vegetable spray. Drizzle with half the melted chocolate. Cover with the remaining bread mixture and drizzle with the remaining chocolate. Bake for 40 to 45 minutes, or until the edges of the bread are light golden and a knife inserted in the center comes out clean. Allow to cool slightly, then chill for at least 2 hours; serve, or cover and keep chilled until ready to serve.

NOTE: If you have a variety of leftover bread—even including raisin bread—that's okay. It can be mixed together and used here.

Classic Rice Pudding

8 to 10 servings

Some things never change—and that's 'cause they're perfect just the way they are. . . .

8 cups (½ gallon) milk
1 cup uncooked long- or
    whole-grain rice

3 egg yolks, beaten
¾ cup sugar
½ teaspoon vanilla extract

In a large pot, combine the milk, rice, egg yolks, and sugar. Bring to a boil over medium heat and cook for 20 to 25 minutes, until thickened and the rice is tender, stirring frequently to keep the rice from sticking. Remove from the heat, stir in the vanilla, and allow to cool slightly. Spoon into a serving bowl or individual dessert dishes and chill for 2 to 3 hours. Serve, or cover and keep chilled until ready to serve.

NOTE: All you need to finish it off just right is a generous dollop of whipped cream and a sprinkle of nutmeg just before serving.

Ambrosia Tapioca Pudding

6 to 8 servings

Make this as a go-along side salad or, better yet, serve it as a light, refreshing dessert.

⅓ cup sugar
3 tablespoons tapioca (see Note)
2¾ cups milk
1 egg, beaten
1 teaspoon vanilla extract

1 can (11 ounces) mandarin oranges, drained
1 can (8 ounces) crushed pineapple, drained
½ cup miniature marshmallows

In a medium-sized saucepan, combine the sugar, tapioca, milk, and egg; let stand for 5 minutes. Cook over medium heat, stirring constantly, for 8 to 10 minutes, or until the mixture comes to a rolling boil. Remove from the heat, stir in the vanilla, and let cool for 20 minutes. Gently stir in the oranges, pineapple, and marsh-mallows. Pour into a serving bowl or individual dessert bowls and chill for at least 2 hours, or until thoroughly chilled. Serve, or cover and keep chilled until ready to serve.

NOTE: Any type of tapioca, including instant, works well in this pudding.

Caramel Vanilla Pudding Surprise

6 to 8 servings

Perk up plain old pudding with the unexpected . . . it's a no-fuss fancy that tastes like "puddin' on the Ritz"!

1 can (15 ounces) apricot halves, drained
1 package (6-serving size) instant vanilla pudding and pie filling, prepared according to the package directions

¼ cup sugar

Place the apricot halves cut side down in the bottom of 6 to 8 individual dessert bowls. Spoon the pudding evenly over the apricot halves. In a small saucepan, melt and cook the sugar over medium heat, stirring, for 4 to 6 minutes, or until light brown and caramelized. Spoon evenly over the pudding. Cover and chill overnight before serving.

NOTE: You could really serve this as soon as it chills completely, but it's best eaten the day after it's made so that the caramelized sugar has turned into a rich caramel sauce.

Black-and-White Napoleon Pudding

When I first tasted this recipe, I was really impressed 'cause I figured it must be really complicated. So, how come it's here? 'Cause it only *tastes* complicated!

1 package (4-serving size) instant vanilla pudding and pie filling, prepared according to the package directions
1 container (12 ounces) frozen whipped topping, thawed

1 package (16 ounces) chocolate-flavored graham crackers
1 container (16 ounces) ready-to-spread chocolate frosting

In a medium-sized bowl, combine the pudding and whipped topping. Place a single layer of graham crackers in the bottom of a 9" × 13" baking dish. Top with one quarter of the pudding mixture. Repeat the layers of graham crackers and pudding 3 more times, and end with another layer of graham crackers. Spread the frosting over the top, then cover and chill overnight to allow the graham crackers to soften. Cut into squares and serve.

NOTE: Black and white or white and black—you can make it either way. So, maybe you'll wanna try this with regular graham crackers, chocolate pudding, and white frosting. Go ahead!

Maple Walnut Mousse

6 to 8 servings

When I was growing up, one of my favorite flavors of ice cream was maple walnut. Now it's one of my favorite flavors of mousse!

1 envelope (0.25 ounce) unflavored
    gelatin
¼ cup cold water
1 cup boiling water

1 cup pure maple syrup
1 cup (½ pint) heavy cream
1 cup chopped walnuts

In a large bowl, sprinkle the gelatin over the cold water and let stand for 5 minutes. Add the boiling water and stir until the gelatin dissolves. Stir in the maple syrup, then cover and chill for about 1½ hours, or until thickened but not set. In a medium-sized bowl, with an electric beater on medium speed, beat the cream until stiff peaks form. Fold the cream into the gelatin mixture, then add the walnuts and continue to fold until well combined. Spoon into a large serving bowl or individual parfait glasses and chill for at least 2 hours. Serve, or cover and keep chilled until ready to serve.

NOTE: Wanna get a little nutty? Top each serving with some additional chopped walnuts.

Minty Mousse

6 to 8 servings

Make the end of a meal really stand out—serve mousse instead of pudding. Its richer texture makes every spoonful scrumptious and luxurious.

1 package (6 ounces) white baking
   bars, broken up
2 cups (1 pint) heavy cream, divided

1½ teaspoons mint extract
⅓ cup confectioners' sugar
8 drops green food color

In a medium-sized saucepan, combine the baking bars and ½ cup heavy cream over low heat, stirring constantly until the bars are melted and the mixture is smooth. Stir in the mint extract, then remove from the heat and let cool completely. In a medium-sized bowl, with an electric beater on medium speed, beat the sugar and the remaining 1½ cups cream until stiff peaks form. Add the food color and beat just until the mixture is uniform in color. Gently fold in the white chocolate mixture until well blended. Cover and chill for at least 2 hours before serving.

NOTE: To really wow the gang, serve this in Special Occasion Chocolate Cups (page 162), each topped with a chocolate-covered thin mint candy.

Strawberry Pretzel Bars

12 to 15 servings

This is a unique combination that started out as a mistake and became a thumbs-up winner!

2 cups finely crushed pretzels
¾ cup (1½ sticks) butter, melted
1 cup plus 3 tablespoons sugar
2 packages (4 servings each) strawberry-flavored gelatin
2 cups boiling water

1 package (20 ounces) frozen strawberries (see Note)
1 package (8 ounces) cream cheese, softened
1 container (12 ounces) frozen whipped topping, thawed

Preheat the oven to 400°F. In a medium-sized bowl, combine the crushed pretzels, butter, and 3 tablespoons sugar. Press into the bottom of a 9" × 13" baking dish that has been coated with non-stick baking spray. Bake for 8 minutes; let cool. In a large bowl, dissolve the gelatin in the boiling water. Add the strawberries and chill until slightly thickened. In another large bowl, with an electric beater on medium speed, combine the cream cheese and the remaining 1 cup sugar until smooth and creamy. Fold in the whipped topping and spread evenly over the pretzel crust. With an electric beater on low speed, beat the gelatin and strawberries until the berries are broken up. Spread over the cream cheese layer. Cover and chill for at least 4 hours, or until firm.

NOTE: Although the strawberries need to be thawed slightly so that they are not frozen solid, the colder they are, the faster the gelatin will thicken.

Cherry Surprise

6 to 8 servings

Three cheers for cherries . . . and for this recipe, too, 'cause it's bursting with sweet cherry flavor.

1 package (4-serving size)
   cherry-flavored gelatin
1 cup boiling water
½ cup cold water

Ice cubes
1¾ cups frozen whipped topping,
   thawed, divided
24 maraschino cherries, well drained

In a medium-sized bowl, dissolve the gelatin in the boiling water. Place the cold water in a 1-cup measuring cup and add enough ice cubes to make 1 cup. Add to the gelatin, stirring until the ice melts. Chill for about 1 hour, or until slightly thickened. With an electric beater on low speed, beat the gelatin and 1¼ cups whipped topping for 2 to 3 minutes, until fluffy. Pour half of the gelatin mixture evenly into 6 to 8 custard cups or dessert bowls. Place a dollop of the remaining ½ cup whipped topping over each. Top each with an equal amount of cherries, then cover with the remaining whipped gelatin mixture, covering the whipped topping and cherries completely. Cover and chill for 2 to 3 hours, or until set.

NOTE: These can also be unmolded for serving by dipping each custard cup in hot water three quarters of the way up the sides for 10 seconds, then inverting quickly onto a dessert plate. Shake gently to loosen each from its cup.

Orange Cocktail Cream

12 to 14 servings

Light and airy, this is the perfect dessert when everyone says they really can't eat anymore. (Wanna bet?!)

2 packages (4 servings each)
  lemon-flavored gelatin
1½ cups boiling water
¾ cup orange juice
Ice cubes
2 teaspoons grated orange peel
  (see Note)

1 container (8 ounces) frozen
  whipped topping, thawed
1 can (30 ounces) fruit cocktail,
  drained

In a large bowl, dissolve the gelatin in the boiling water. Place the orange juice in a 2-cup measuring cup and add enough ice cubes to make 1¾ cups. Add to the gelatin along with the grated orange peel, stirring until the ice melts and the gelatin thickens slightly. Add the whipped topping and, with an electric beater or large whisk, beat until completely blended. Add the fruit cocktail and stir until well combined. Spoon into a 10-inch tube pan. Cover and chill overnight, until set. When ready to serve, dip the tube pan in hot water three quarters of the way up the sides for 10 seconds, then invert quickly onto a serving platter that is larger than the pan. Shake gently to loosen from the pan.

NOTE: Grated citrus peel is often called zest. It's the flavorful colored outside part of the citrus skin. You can grate the citrus skin to get the zest, or it can be removed with a gadget called a zester that's designed to remove the thin skin without going too deep and getting the bitter white skin, or pith.

Pot of Gold

12 to 14 servings

It's said that at the end of every rainbow there's a pot of gold. Why not have one at the end of a special meal, too? (When you make it yourself, it's guaranteed!)

1 package (4-serving size)
   strawberry-flavored gelatin
1 package (4-serving size)
   orange-flavored gelatin
3 cups boiling water, divided
1 cup cold water, divided
1 package (4-serving size)
   lemon-flavored gelatin

¼ cup sugar
½ cup orange juice
1 can (8 ounces) pineapple tidbits,
   drained
1 container (8 ounces) frozen
   whipped topping, thawed

Prepare the strawberry and orange gelatins separately by dissolving each in 1 cup boiling water; stir until completely dissolved. Add ½ cup cold water to each, then pour each into a separate 8-inch square pan. Chill for about 1½ hours, or until set, then cut into ½-inch cubes. Cover and set aside in the refrigerator. Dissolve the lemon gelatin and sugar in the remaining 1 cup boiling water and stir in the orange juice; chill until slightly thickened, about 30 minutes. Stir in the pineapple tidbits and whipped topping; mix well. Fold in the gelatin cubes and spoon into a 10-inch tube pan. Cover and chill for 6 to 8 hours, or until set. When ready to serve, dip the tube pan three quarters of the way up the sides in hot water for 10 seconds and invert quickly onto a serving plate that is larger than the pan. Gently shake to loosen from the pan.

NOTE: It's fun to use different flavored gelatins to get different color combinations. For example, you can make gelatin cubes of strawberry and lime for a Christmas Pot of Gold!

Tropical Gelatin Salad

8 to 12 servings

Each spoonful will make you feel as if you're on a deserted tropical island. The only thing missing is the ocean breeze!

1 package (4-serving size) lime-
flavored gelatin
2 cups boiling water, divided
1 can (12 ounces) lemon-lime soda,
divided
½ cup finely shredded cabbage

1 package (4-serving size)
lemon-flavored gelatin
1 can (8 ounces) crushed pineapple,
undrained
⅓ cup low-fat vanilla yogurt

In a medium-sized bowl, combine the lime gelatin and 1 cup boiling water; stir to dissolve the gelatin. Add ¾ cup of the lemon-lime soda; mix well. Add the cabbage and mix again. Pour the mixture into a 3-quart gelatin mold or a 10-inch Bundt pan and chill for 1 hour, or until set. In a medium-sized bowl, combine the lemon gelatin and the remaining 1 cup boiling water; stir to dissolve the gelatin. Add the remaining ¾ cup soda, the pineapple (juice and all), and the yogurt; whisk until smooth. Pour over the set lime gelatin mixture, cover, and chill for at least 2 hours, or until set. When ready to serve, immerse the bottom of the mold in warm water for a few seconds, then invert onto a flat serving plate larger than the mold and release the mold.

NOTE: No mold? No problem! Just make it in a large serving bowl and serve it right out of the bowl, or unmold it, following the directions above.

Sunburst Gelatin Parfaits

6 servings

Just spoon this together and chill it to come up with a light-tasting, fruity treat that'll be an overnight success!

1 package (4-serving size) lemon-flavored gelatin, mixed according to the package directions
1 package (4-serving size) strawberry-flavored gelatin, mixed according to the package directions

1 cup marshmallow creme
1 tablespoon orange juice
1 tablespoon lemon juice

In an 8-inch square baking dish, combine 1 cup of the lemon gelatin with ½ cup of the strawberry gelatin; stir together to make orange-colored gelatin. Pour the remaining lemon and strawberry gelatin into separate 8-inch square or 7" × 11" glass baking dishes. Chill for 4 to 5 hours, or until set. Cut into ½-inch cubes. Spoon the red gelatin cubes evenly into 6 parfait glasses. Repeat with the orange and yellow gelatin cubes. In a small bowl, combine the marshmallow creme, orange juice, and lemon juice, mixing until smooth. Spoon evenly over each parfait and serve, or cover and chill until ready to serve.

Blueberry Lime Mold

10 to 12 servings

Tangy lime flavor and crunchy fresh blueberries—what could be more refreshing and colorful?!

1 package (4-serving size) lime-
   flavored gelatin
1 tablespoon sugar
2 tablespoons lime juice

1½ cups boiling water
1 container (8 ounces) frozen
   whipped topping, thawed
1 pint fresh blueberries (see Note)

In a medium-sized bowl, combine the gelatin, sugar, lime juice, and boiling water, stirring until the gelatin and sugar are dissolved. Chill for about 1 hour, or until slightly thickened. With an electric beater on high speed, beat the gelatin until light-colored and doubled in volume. Beat in the whipped topping, then gently fold in the blueberries. Pour into a 4- to 5-cup gelatin mold. Cover and chill for 3 to 4 hours, or until firm. Dip the mold in warm water and unmold onto a large serving platter.

NOTE: Frozen blueberries can also be used, but be sure to drain them really well.

Waldorf Gelatin

5 to 6 servings

The name tells the story—like the famous salad, this gelatin version is chock-full of apples and walnuts.

1¼ cups apple juice, divided
1 package (4-serving size) strawberry-flavored gelatin
Ice cubes

1 medium-sized apple, cored, peeled, and finely chopped
2 medium-sized bananas, sliced
2 tablespoons chopped walnuts

In a small saucepan, bring ¾ cup apple juice to a boil over medium heat. In a large bowl, combine the boiling apple juice and the gelatin, stirring until the gelatin is completely dissolved. Place the remaining ½ cup apple juice in a 1-cup measuring cup and add enough ice cubes to make 1 cup. Add to the gelatin, stirring until the ice is melted and the gelatin is slightly thickened. Stir in the apple, bananas, and walnuts. Spoon into individual dessert dishes or a large serving bowl. Cover and chill for 2 hours, or until firm.

NOTE: This makes a great dessert, but you can also serve it on a bed of shredded lettuce for a light lunch salad.

Summer Citrus "Pie"

8 to 10 servings

A fan sent me this recipe for a citrus dessert that's kind of like a crustless pie. It's so different and yummy, I had to share it with you.

1 package (4-serving size)
   lime-flavored gelatin
1 cup boiling water
½ cup half-and-half

½ teaspoon vanilla extract
½ cup sour cream
1 cup sliced strawberries
1 teaspoon grated lemon peel

In a medium-sized bowl, dissolve the gelatin in the boiling water. Gradually stir in the half-and-half and vanilla. Add the sour cream; mix well. (The mixture will appear curdled.) Chill for 15 to 20 minutes, until slightly thickened. With an electric beater, beat until the mixture is smooth, then stir in the strawberries and grated lemon peel. Pour into a 9-inch pie plate, cover, and chill for 3 hours, or until set.

Lemony Fruit Tart

6 to 8 servings

Looking for a dessert that's perfectly light for after a big meal? Here it is!

1 sheet frozen puff pastry, thawed (½ of a 17¼-ounce package)
1 package (4-serving size) instant lemon pudding and pie filling, prepared according to the package directions

1 pint fresh strawberries, sliced

Preheat the oven to 400°F. On a lightly floured surface, roll out the puff pastry to a 10" × 15" rectangle. With a sharp knife, cut a 1-inch-wide strip from each of the 2 long sides. Brush the edges of the 2 strips lightly with water and place each strip on top of the edge it was cut from, forming a rim (see illustration 1). Do the same for the short sides, forming a rim around the whole pastry (see illustration 2). With a fork, pierce the pastry all over, except for the rim.

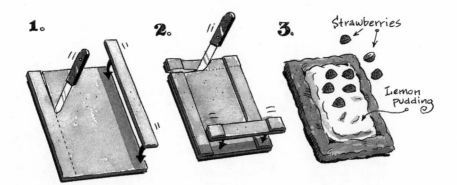

1.   2.   3.   Strawberries

Lemon Pudding

Place on a rimmed baking sheet and bake for 16 to 18 minutes, or until golden. Remove from the oven and allow to cool; if the center has puffed, push it down with the back of a fork, leaving the rim intact. Spoon the pudding into the cooled pastry shell and top with the sliced strawberries (see illustration 3). Cover and chill for at least 2 hours, or until ready to serve.

NOTE:No strawberries? Any type of fresh berries, kiwifruit, orange slices, grapes, or even canned fruit such as mandarin oranges can be used.

Fruit

Spirited Fruit Cocktail

8 to 10 servings

This is what I call a true fruit "cocktail" 'cause it gets its zing from the liquor that we put in it. Made as directed, it's for adults only. But if you'd rather make it without alcohol, you can. (See my recipe note.) Either way, why not serve it in stemmed cocktail glasses?

1 cantaloupe, peeled, seeded, and cut into bite-sized pieces

1 pineapple, peeled, cored, and cut into bite-sized pieces

1 pint fresh strawberries, halved

2 cups seedless red grapes

⅓ cup slivered almonds, toasted (see Note, page 6)

⅓ cup Triple Sec or other orange-flavored liqueur

2 tablespoons light or dark rum

2 tablespoons sugar

In a large bowl, toss together the cantaloupe, pineapple, strawberries, grapes, and almonds. In a small bowl, combine the Triple Sec, rum, and sugar; pour over the fruit and toss until well coated. Cover and chill for at least 3 hours before serving.

NOTE: If you prefer to make this without alcohol, just substitute ½ cup orange juice for the Triple Sec and rum.

Harvest Fruit Compote

8 to 12 servings

What a rich, flavorful combination of fresh harvesttime fruit! And with such great taste, who'd ever think it's low-fat?!

5 medium-sized apples, cored and
   cut into 1-inch chunks
3 medium-sized pears, cored and
   cut into 1-inch chunks
3 large oranges, peeled and
   sectioned

1 package (12 ounces) fresh
   cranberries
1½ cups apple juice
1½ cups firmly packed light brown
   sugar

In a large pot, combine all the ingredients and bring to a boil over medium-high heat. Reduce the heat to medium and cook for 10 to 15 minutes, or until the fruit is tender, stirring occasionally. Chill until the fruit has cooled, then spoon into an airtight container and keep chilled until ready to serve.

Fruit Toss

6 to 8 servings

There's nothing fancy about this—just toss and chill for a juicy-sweet snack or dessert!

1 can (20 ounces) pineapple chunks, drained
1 can (16 ounces) peach halves, drained and cut into 1-inch chunks (see Note)
1 jar (10 ounces) maraschino cherries, drained and halved

1 cup chopped pecans
2 cups (1 pint) half-and-half
¼ cup sugar
2 teaspoons lemon juice
¼ teaspoon vanilla extract

In a large bowl, combine all the ingredients and toss until well mixed. Cover and chill for at least 3 hours before serving.

NOTE: Any kind of canned fruit, such as pears, apricots, or fruit cocktail, can be used.

Light 'n' Easy Ambrosia

6 to 8 servings

Lower in fat than traditional ambrosia, but every bit as high in flavor. See if you agree with me!

1 can (20 ounces) pineapple chunks, drained
1 jar (10 ounces) maraschino cherries, drained and halved

2 cups miniature marshmallows
1 cup low-fat vanilla yogurt
½ cup flaked coconut

In a large bowl, combine all the ingredients and toss until the fruit and marshmallows are evenly coated with the yogurt. Cover and chill for at least 1 hour before serving.

NOTE: This makes a super side dish as well as a nice, light dessert.

Frozen Fruit Salad

8 to 10 servings

A refreshing anytime treat, icy-cool fruit salad always goes down easy. And done this way . . . a masterpiece!

1 cup sour cream
1 cup frozen whipped topping, thawed
¼ cup sugar
1 teaspoon vanilla extract
1 can (20 ounces) crushed pineapple, drained and squeezed dry

1 can (16½ ounces) dark sweet cherries, quartered and well drained (see Note)
2 medium-sized bananas, cut into ¼-inch-thick slices
½ cup chopped walnuts

In a medium-sized bowl, combine the sour cream, whipped topping, sugar, and vanilla. Gently fold in the pineapple, cherries, bananas, and walnuts. Line a 9" × 5" loaf pan with plastic wrap, making sure the plastic wrap extends over the edges. Spoon the fruit mixture into the loaf pan, cover, and freeze overnight. When ready to serve, invert the loaf onto a serving plate and remove the plastic wrap, then slice.

NOTE: After draining the cherries, place them on paper towels until the excess liquid is absorbed.

Chocolate-Laced Fruit Kebabs

10 kebabs

Say good-bye to plain old fruit salad and hello to a fancy-looking, fancy-tasting dessert or pick-me-up.

10 wooden or metal skewers
   (each 10 to 12 inches long)
20 medium-sized strawberries, hulled
20 chunks of honeydew
   (about ½ of a large honeydew)
20 chunks of cantaloupe
   (about ½ of a large cantaloupe)

20 chunks of fresh pineapple
   (about ½ of a large pineapple)
½ cup (3 ounces) semisweet
   chocolate chips
1 tablespoon butter
2 tablespoons light corn syrup

On each of the skewers, alternate a strawberry, honeydew chunk, cantaloupe chunk, and pineapple chunk; repeat. Place on a waxed paper–lined cookie sheet. In a small saucepan, combine the chocolate chips, butter, and corn syrup over low heat; stir until the chips are melted. Drizzle the chocolate mixture evenly over the fruit on each skewer. Chill until the chocolate hardens, then cover loosely with plastic wrap and keep chilled until ready to serve.

NOTE: Not in the mood for chocolate? Make the fruit skewers and have them without chocolate as a healthy snack or even a great edible garnish.

Raspberry Baked Apples

6 servings

If only Mom had made me baked apples like these. . . .

6 large baking apples, cored
⅓ cup raspberry liqueur, divided
⅓ cup firmly packed light brown
    sugar

2 teaspoons vanilla extract
¼ teaspoon ground cinnamon
1 cup frozen whipped topping,
    thawed

Preheat the oven to 325°F. Place the apples in a medium-sized baking dish. In a small bowl, combine the liqueur, brown sugar, vanilla, and cinnamon. Spoon the mixture into the center and over the top of each apple. Bake for 40 to 45 minutes, or until the apples are tender and can be pierced easily with a knife. Allow to cool slightly, then chill until completely cooled. When ready to serve, remove the apples to a rimmed platter. Add the whipped topping to the sauce in the baking dish, stirring until well blended. Serve the apples topped with the sauce.

NOTE: A fancy way to serve these is to slice each apple into wedges and drizzle with some additional raspberry liqueur.

Pears Romanoff

6 servings

When we really want to make the gang feel special, we need an elegant easy like this one!

3 pears, halved and cored
1 tablespoon light brown sugar
1 package (3 ounces) cream cheese, softened
2 tablespoons granulated sugar

3 tablespoons milk
½ teaspoon vanilla extract
¼ teaspoon ground cinnamon
¼ teaspoon ground ginger

Preheat the oven to 400°F. Place the pears cut side up in a 9" × 13" baking dish and sprinkle with the brown sugar. Cover with aluminum foil and bake for 25 to 30 minutes, or until tender; let cool. In a small bowl, with an electric beater on medium speed, beat the cream cheese and granulated sugar until creamy. Add the milk, vanilla, cinnamon, and ginger; beat for 3 to 4 minutes, until smooth. Place the pears on a serving platter and drizzle with the cream cheese mixture. Cover loosely and chill for at least 2 hours before serving.

Baked Pine-Apple

8 to 10 servings

What's the best part of a pie? The filling, of course. So c'mon and dig into this crustless pie. And when it's served with a scoop of vanilla or maple walnut ice cream, you get a double winner!

6 apples, peeled, cored, and cut into
    wedges (see Note)
1 can (8 ounces) crushed pineapple,
    undrained

1 can (6 ounces) pineapple juice
⅓ cup chopped walnuts
2 tablespoons dark brown sugar
½ teaspoon ground cinnamon

Preheat the oven to 350°F. In a large bowl, combine the apples, the undrained pineapple, and the pineapple juice. Spoon into a 9-inch deep-dish pie plate that has been coated with nonstick vegetable spray. Sprinkle with the walnuts, brown sugar, and cinnamon. Bake for 45 to 50 minutes, or until the apples are tender. Allow to cool slightly, then chill for at least 3 hours before serving.

NOTE: The more tart the apples in here, the better!

Peaches and Almond Cream

4 servings

If you're a peach lover like I am, you're in for quite a treat. Maybe you should make a double batch, since this seems to be a favorite of just about everybody!

½ cup milk
2 tablespoons sugar
1½ teaspoons cornstarch
¾ teaspoon vanilla extract

¼ teaspoon almond extract
½ cup heavy cream
4 peaches, pitted and cut into
    wedges (see Note)

In a small saucepan, combine the milk, sugar, and cornstarch over medium-high heat. Bring to a boil, then reduce the heat to low and simmer, stirring, until thickened. Remove from the heat and allow to cool completely, then add the vanilla and almond extracts. In a medium-sized bowl, with an electric beater on medium speed, beat the cream until stiff peaks form. Fold in the milk mixture. Place the cut peaches in 4 individual dessert dishes or a large serving bowl and top with the cream sauce. Cover loosely and chill for at least 1 hour before serving.

NOTE: If fresh peaches aren't in season, well-drained canned peaches can certainly be substituted.

Baked Pear Tart

6 to 8 servings

This one is sure to please, so put on the coffee and invite the gang over!

1 sheet frozen puff pastry, thawed (½ of a 17½-ounce package)
4 large ripe pears, peeled, cored, and thinly sliced (see Note)
¼ cup granulated sugar

1 teaspoon ground cinnamon
½ cup sour cream
¼ cup firmly packed light brown sugar

Preheat the oven to 375°F. On a lightly floured surface, roll out the puff pastry to a 10" × 15" rectangle. Place on a rimmed baking sheet. Lay the pear slices on the dough, slightly overlapping the slices and covering the entire surface of the dough. In a small bowl, combine the granulated sugar and cinnamon and sprinkle over the pears. Bake for 40 to 45 minutes, or until the pastry is golden; allow to cool. In a small bowl, combine the sour cream and brown sugar, then gently spread over the tart. Cover loosely and keep chilled until ready to serve.

NOTE: No pears? Don't worry, apples taste just as good with this!

Cakes

Chocolate Strawberry Dream Cake

12 to 16 servings

I first tried this at one of our monthly office birthday parties. We all thought it was so good that we've had it *every* month since!

1 package (18.25 ounces) chocolate cake mix, batter prepared according to the package directions
1 package (4-serving size) instant chocolate pudding and pie filling

1½ cups cold milk
1 cup sliced fresh strawberries
1 container (8 ounces) frozen whipped topping, thawed

Bake the cake batter according to the package directions for two 9-inch round layers; let cool. In a medium-sized bowl, with an electric beater on medium speed, beat the pudding mix and milk until well mixed; allow to thicken slightly. Invert 1 cake layer onto a serving plate. Spread 1 cup of the pudding over the cake layer and cover with the sliced strawberries. In a medium-sized bowl, combine the remaining pudding with the whipped topping until thoroughly blended. Place the second cake layer over the strawberries, then frost the top and sides of the cake with the whipped topping mixture. Chill for at least 2 hours; serve, or cover loosely and keep chilled until ready to serve.

NOTE: Be sure to give this cake its domed look by placing the top layer of cake rounded side up.

Cassata Cake

12 to 16 servings

How 'bout having an Italian feast—a little antipasto, some pasta with sauce, and, of course, this classic Italian dessert? Well, what are you waiting for?!

1 package (18.25 ounces) yellow cake mix, batter prepared according to the package directions
1 container (15 ounces) ricotta cheese
1 cup (6 ounces) miniature semisweet chocolate chips
¼ cup plus 2 tablespoons granulated sugar, divided

1 teaspoon vanilla extract
¼ teaspoon ground cinnamon
2 tablespoons dark rum
¼ cup water
1 cup (½ pint) heavy cream
2 tablespoons confectioners' sugar
1 cup sliced almonds, toasted (see Note)

Bake the cake batter according to the package directions for two 9-inch round layers; let cool, then remove from the pans. Meanwhile, in a medium-sized bowl, combine the ricotta cheese, chocolate chips, ¼ cup granulated sugar, the vanilla, and cinnamon; mix well, then cover and chill. In a small bowl, combine the rum, water, and the remaining 2 tablespoons granulated sugar; mix, then set aside. Place 1 cake layer on a serving platter and drizzle with the rum mixture. Cover with the ricotta cheese mixture and top with the second cake layer. In a medium-sized bowl, with an electric beater on high speed, beat the heavy cream and confectioners' sugar until stiff peaks form. Frost the top and sides of the cake with the whipped cream and sprinkle the top and sides with the toasted almonds. Cover loosely and chill for at least 2 hours before serving.

NOTE: To toast the almonds, place them on a rimmed baking sheet in a single layer and bake in a preheated 350°F. oven for 1 to 2 minutes, just until golden. They toast very quickly, so watch them carefully to avoid burning!

Butternut Squash Roll

8 to 10 servings

Don't tell anybody, but this sweet cake has a secret ingredient from the veggie garden. That's how you know it'll "grow" on your whole gang!

¾ cup all-purpose flour
1 teaspoon baking powder
2 teaspoons ground cinnamon
1 teaspoon ground ginger
½ teaspoon ground nutmeg
½ teaspoon salt
3 eggs
1 cup granulated sugar
1 package (11 ounces) frozen
    butternut squash, thawed and
    drained

1½ teaspoons vanilla extract, divided
1 cup confectioners' sugar, plus extra
    for sprinkling
1 package (8 ounces) cream cheese,
    softened
¼ cup (½ stick) butter, softened

Preheat the oven to 375°F. In a medium-sized bowl, combine the flour, baking powder, cinnamon, ginger, nutmeg, and salt; mix well and set aside. In a large bowl, with an electric beater on high speed, beat the eggs for 4 to 5 minutes, until fluffy. Beat in the granulated sugar, squash, and 1 teaspoon vanilla. Fold in the flour mixture until well blended. Pour the batter onto a rimmed 10" × 15" baking sheet that has been coated with nonstick baking spray. Bake for 12 to 15 minutes, or until a wooden toothpick inserted in the center comes out clean. Remove from the oven and invert onto a clean kitchen towel that has been sprinkled with confectioners' sugar. While the cake is still hot, roll it up in the towel jelly-roll style from a narrow end; cool on a wire rack. When cool, unroll the cake and remove the towel. In a small bowl, with an electric beater on medium speed, beat the 1 cup confectioners' sugar, the cream cheese, butter, and the remaining ½ teaspoon vanilla until creamy. Spread over the top of the cake, then roll it up again. Chill for at least 2 hours. When ready to serve, sprinkle the roll with confectioners' sugar, then cut into ½-inch-thick slices.

NOTE: You might want to serve these sprinkled with some additional cinnamon . . . I do!

Buttermilk Carrot Cake

12 to 16 servings

So many of us have a favorite carrot cake recipe, but the buttermilk really makes *this* recipe rise to the top!

2 cups all-purpose flour
2 teaspoons baking powder
2 teaspoons baking soda
1 tablespoon ground cinnamon
½ teaspoon ground allspice
½ teaspoon salt
1 pound carrots, shredded
   (about 2 cups)
1 can (8 ounces) crushed pineapple,
   drained

2 cups firmly packed light brown
   sugar
1 cup finely chopped walnuts
4 eggs
½ cup buttermilk
½ cup vegetable oil
Buttery Cream Cheese Frosting
   (next page)

Preheat the oven to 350°F. In a medium-sized bowl, combine the flour, baking powder, baking soda, cinnamon, allspice, and salt; mix well. In a large bowl, combine the remaining ingredients except the frosting. Stir in the flour mixture until well combined. Divide the batter between two 9-inch round cake pans that have been coated with nonstick baking spray. Bake for 35 to 40 minutes, or until a wooden toothpick inserted in the center comes out clean. Let cool for 10 minutes, then invert onto racks to cool completely. Meanwhile, prepare the Buttery Cream Cheese Frosting. Place 1 cake layer upside down on a serving plate and frost the top. Place the second layer over the first and frost the top and sides. Cover loosely and chill for at least 3 hours before serving.

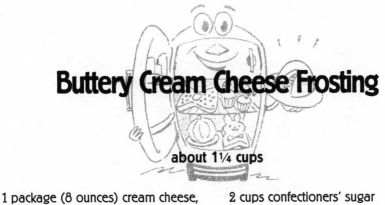

Buttery Cream Cheese Frosting

about 1¼ cups

1 package (8 ounces) cream cheese, softened

½ cup (1 stick) unsalted butter, softened

2 cups confectioners' sugar

In a large bowl, with an electric beater on medium speed, beat the cream cheese and butter until creamy. Gradually add the confectioners' sugar, beating for 1 to 2 minutes, until smooth. Use immediately, or cover and chill until ready to use. Bring to room temperature before using.

NOTE: Top the frosted cake with a little grated carrot for that fresh-from-the-garden look.

Orange Ring Cake

12 to 16 servings

If the aroma from this cake baking doesn't get you, one forkful will surely have you hooked!

1 box (18.25 ounces) yellow cake mix
½ cup (1 stick) butter, softened
3 eggs
1 cup plus 2 tablespoons orange juice

Grated rind of 2 oranges
1 package (3 ounces) cream cheese, softened
¼ cup confectioners' sugar

In a large bowl, with an electric beater on medium speed, combine the cake mix, butter, eggs, 1 cup orange juice, and the orange rind. Beat for 2 minutes, until well mixed. Pour the batter into a 10-inch Bundt or tube pan that has been coated with nonstick baking spray. Bake for 40 to 45 minutes, or until a wooden toothpick inserted in the center comes out clean. Remove from the oven and cool for 10 minutes, then invert onto a wire rack to cool completely before placing on a serving platter. In a medium-sized bowl, with an electric beater on medium speed, beat the cream cheese, confectioners' sugar, and the remaining 2 tablespoons orange juice for 2 to 3 minutes, until smooth. Spoon over the top of the cake, allowing it to drip down the sides. Cover loosely and chill for at least 3 hours before serving.

Lemon Macadamia Cake

12 to 16 servings

With a few of your own touches, they'll never know you started this with a cake mix!

1 teaspoon grated lemon peel
1 package (18.25 ounces) lemon cake mix, batter prepared according to the package directions
1 jar (7 ounces) macadamia nuts, coarsely chopped, divided (see Note)

1 can (15¾ ounces) lemon pie filling, divided
1 cup (½ pint) heavy cream
2 tablespoons sugar

Stir the lemon peel into the cake batter and pour the batter into two 9-inch round cake pans per the package directions; sprinkle ¼ cup chopped nuts over the top of each and bake according to the package directions. When cooled completely, unmold 1 cake layer onto a serv-ing plate. Reserve ½ cup of the lemon pie filling and place the remaining pie filling in a medium-sized bowl; add ½ cup chopped nuts and spread over the cake layer. Top with the second cake layer and spoon the reserved lemon pie filling in the center of the top layer; chill. In a medium-sized bowl, with an electric beater on medium speed, beat the cream and sugar until stiff peaks form. Frost the sides of the cake and frost around the filling on the top of the cake. Sprinkle with the remaining chopped nuts and chill for at least 2 hours. Serve, or cover loosely and keep chilled until ready to serve.

NOTE: I think the best way to coarsely chop macadamia nuts is to do it with a chef's knife. That way, the pieces are big enough to really give you something to bite into!

61

Apple Spice Custard Cake

12 to 15 servings

This is no ordinary cake—a perfect holiday treat, its heavenly layer of thick creamy topping covers a spicy but sweet fruit-filled center.

2 medium-sized apples, peeled, cored, and finely chopped (about 2 cups) (see Note)
1 package (18.25 ounces) spice cake mix, batter prepared according to the package directions
1 can (14 ounces) sweetened condensed milk
1 cup sour cream, at room temperature
¼ cup lemon juice
Ground cinnamon for garnish

Stir the apples into the cake batter and bake according to the package directions for a 9" × 13" cake. In a medium-sized bowl, combine the sweetened condensed milk, sour cream, and lemon juice. Spread over the top of the hot cake. Bake for 10 minutes, or until the center of the topping is set, like custard. Sprinkle with cinnamon and cool completely. Cover and chill for at least 2 hours before serving.

NOTE: I prefer to use a tart variety of apple in this, like Granny Smith. But if you'd rather, a Delicious will give you a sweeter taste that really *is* delicious!

Nutty Banana Cake

12 to 15 servings

Don't throw out those starting-to-go-brown bananas! Turn them into this great snacking cake.

¾ cup vegetable shortening

3 cups sugar, divided

3 eggs

6 medium-sized bananas, mashed (about 2 cups)

2 cups chopped pecans

2¼ cups all-purpose flour

6 tablespoons buttermilk

1¼ teaspoons baking soda

3 tablespoons butter

¼ cup milk

½ teaspoon vanilla extract

Preheat the oven to 375°F. In a large bowl, with an electric beater on medium speed, beat the shortening and 2 cups sugar for 1 to 2 minutes, until thoroughly blended. Add the eggs, increase the speed to high, and beat for 2 minutes, or until fluffy. Fold in the bananas and nuts, then fold in the flour, buttermilk, and baking soda. Pour the batter into a 9" × 13" baking pan that has been coated with nonstick baking spray. Bake for 35 to 40 minutes, or until a wooden toothpick inserted in the center comes out clean. Allow to cool in the pan on a wire rack. Meanwhile, in a large saucepan, combine the remaining 1 cup sugar, the butter, and milk. Bring to a boil over medium heat, stirring occasionally; continue cooking for 5 more minutes. Remove from the heat and stir in the vanilla, then allow to cool for 15 to 20 minutes, or until slightly thickened. Spread the sugar syrup over the cake and allow to harden, then cover loosely and chill until ready to serve.

NOTE: This cake can also be cut into squares, then covered in the sugar syrup, to create petit four–like cake squares.

All-American Strawberry Shortcake

10 to 12 servings

This is one to serve to your "berry" best company—a light, fruity cream cake that's long on goodness and short on work.

1 package (18.25 ounces) yellow cake mix, batter prepared according to the package directions
3 pints fresh strawberries, hulled

2 cups (1 pint) heavy cream
1 tablespoon confectioners' sugar
1 teaspoon vanilla extract

Bake the cake batter according to the package directions for two 9-inch round layers; let cool. Slice each cake layer in half horizontally, making 4 layers, and place 1 layer on a serving platter. Slice 2 pints strawberries and set aside. In a large bowl, with an electric beater on high speed, beat the cream, sugar, and vanilla until stiff peaks form. Spread one quarter of the whipped cream mixture over the top of the first cake layer. Top with one third of the sliced strawberries. Repeat with the remaining layers, topping the final layer with the remaining pint of whole strawberries, hulled side down. Cover loosely and chill for at least 2 hours before serving.

NOTE: You can bake the cake layers ahead of time and freeze them until needed. Just make sure to wrap each layer well.

Coconut Dream Cake

12 to 16 servings

If you're dreaming of a tropical-tasting treat that's a balmy breeze to bake . . . look no further.

1 package (12 ounces) fresh-frozen unsweetened grated coconut, thawed, divided (see Note)
1 package (18.25 ounces) white cake mix, batter prepared according to the package directions
1 cup (2 sticks) unsalted butter, softened
2 cups confectioners' sugar
1 package (6 ounces) white baking bars, melted

Add 2 cups of the coconut to the batter and mix until thoroughly combined. Bake according to the package directions for two 9-inch round layers; let cool completely. In a large bowl, with an electric beater on medium speed, beat the butter, confectioners' sugar, and the melted white baking bars until fluffy and doubled in volume. Add the remaining coconut and mix until thoroughly combined. Place 1 cake layer upside down on a serving platter and frost the top. Place the second layer over the first and frost the top and sides. Cover loosely and chill for at least 2 hours before serving.

NOTE: Flaked coconut can also be used, but since it's already sweetened, you may want to cut back on the amount of confectioners' sugar in the frosting.

Traditional Boston Cream Pie

8 to 10 servings

No, no, no, this dessert isn't in the wrong chapter. I know its name says it's a pie, but it's really more like a cake. There's something else I know—whatever it's called and wherever it goes, it is sooo good!!

1 box (18.25 ounces) yellow cake mix, batter prepared according to the package directions
1 package (4-serving size) instant vanilla pudding and pie filling

1 cup cold milk
Chocolate Glaze (next page)

Bake the cake batter according to the package directions for two 8-inch layers; let cool. Reserve 1 cake layer for another use (see Note). Slice the remaining cake layer in half horizontally and place the bottom half cut side up on a serving plate. In a medium-sized bowl, whisk the pudding mix and milk together until the pudding is thick and smooth; spread the pudding over the bottom cake layer. Place the other half of the cake layer cut side down over the pudding. Refrigerate while you prepare the Chocolate Glaze. Allow the glaze to cool slightly before spreading it over the top of the cake. Chill the glazed cake for at least 1 hour, until the filling and glaze are set. Serve, or cover loosely and keep chilled until ready to serve.

NOTE: Traditional Boston Cream Pie isn't a traditional pie with a crust; it's a round layer cake with a custard filling. And because this one starts with a cake mix, you're going to have a second cake layer that you don't need this time. So, you can either make two pies now or freeze the second cake layer to make another pie. This is so creamy good that I bet you'll use it soon!

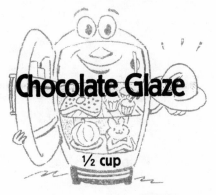

Chocolate Glaze

½ cup

¼ cup sugar
2 teaspoons cornstarch
⅓ cup water

½ ounce (½ square) unsweetened chocolate
½ teaspoon vanilla extract

In a small saucepan, combine the sugar, cornstarch, water, and chocolate over low heat. Cook, stirring constantly, until the chocolate is melted and the mixture is thickened, bubbly, and smooth. Remove from the heat and stir in the vanilla. Cool slightly before using.

NOTE: Don't be afraid to top any cake with this glaze. Remember, there are no rules!

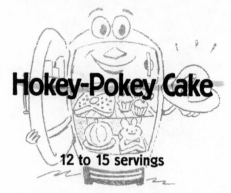

Hokey-Pokey Cake

12 to 15 servings

Put your spoon in, take your spoon out, fill the cake with pudding, and serve it all about!

1 package (18.25 ounces) chocolate cake mix, batter prepared according to the package directions

2 packages (4 servings each) instant pistachio pudding and pie filling
½ cup confectioners' sugar
3½ cups cold milk

Bake the cake batter according to the package directions for a 9" × 13" cake. Remove the cake from the oven and while still warm, poke holes into the cake at 1-inch intervals with the handle of a wooden spoon; set aside. In a large bowl, with an electric beater on low speed, beat the pudding mix, sugar, and milk until thoroughly combined. The mixture should be loose; do not overbeat. Before the mixture thickens, pour half evenly over the warm cake, making sure it runs into the holes. Chill the remaining pudding for about 10 minutes, allowing it to thicken slightly, then spoon over the top of the cake. Chill for at least 2 hours, then serve, or cover and keep chilled until ready to serve.

NOTE: Although this cake can be made with a variety of different flavors of cake and pudding mixes, I've found that the chocolate-pistachio version not only tastes great, but also looks great.

Cheesecakes

White Chocolate Macadamia Cheesecake

12 to 14 servings

If it's time to show off your cheesecake "smarts," you've turned to the right page. After just one forkful, they'll think you're a pro!

1 jar (7 ounces) macadamia nuts, divided
1 cup plus 2 tablespoons sugar, divided
1 cup graham cracker crumbs
¼ cup (½ stick) butter, melted

3 packages (8 ounces each) cream cheese, softened
2 eggs
¾ cup sour cream
2 packages (6 ounces each) white baking bars, melted

Preheat the oven to 350°F. In a blender or food processor that has been fitted with its metal cutting blade, finely chop ½ cup macadamia nuts with 2 tablespoons sugar. Place in a medium-sized bowl and add the graham cracker crumbs and melted butter; mix well. Press into the bottom of a 10-inch springform pan. In a large bowl, with an electric beater on medium speed, beat the cream cheese, the remaining 1 cup sugar, and the eggs until smooth. Add the sour cream, then the melted white baking bars, mixing until well combined after each addition. With a knife, coarsely chop the remaining macadamia nuts and stir into the cream cheese mixture. Pour over the crust and bake for 45 to 50 minutes, until almost set in the center. Turn off the oven and leave the cheesecake in the oven with the door ajar for 1 hour. Remove from the oven and allow to cool completely, then cover and chill for at least 4 hours, or overnight.

NOTE: For even more pizzazz, garnish the top with some dark-chocolate–dipped macadamia nuts.

71

German Black Bottom Cheesecake

8 to 10 servings

Just when you thought you knew what to expect with German Chocolate Cake, I've gone and given it a new twist. What's the twist? Now it's got a Chocolate Cheesecake bottom. It can't get better than this!

2 packages (8 ounces each)
   cream cheese, softened
½ cup plus ⅓ cup sugar, divided
3 eggs
1 package (4 ounces) German® sweet
   chocolate bar, melted
1½ teaspoons vanilla extract, divided

One 9-inch chocolate graham cracker
   pie crust
1 can (5 ounces) evaporated milk
¼ cup (½ stick) butter
½ cup flaked coconut
½ cup chopped pecans

Preheat the oven to 350°F. In a large bowl, with an electric beater on medium speed, beat the cream cheese and ½ cup sugar until well blended. Add 2 eggs one at a time, mixing well after each addition. Blend in the melted chocolate and 1 teaspoon vanilla, then pour the mixture into the pie crust. Bake for 35 to 40 minutes, or until firm; let cool for 15 to 20 minutes. In a small bowl, whisk the remaining egg until lightly beaten. Place in a small saucepan and add the evaporated milk, butter, and the remaining ⅓ cup sugar and ½ teaspoon vanilla; heat over medium-low heat for 12 to 15 minutes, or until thickened, stirring constantly. Stir in the coconut and pecans; let cool. Spread over the top of the cheesecake; cover and chill for at least 4 hours before serving.

NOTE: German® sweet chocolate can be found in the baking section of your supermarket, near the other baking chocolate.

Tasty Toffee Cheesecake

8 to 10 servings

When I can't quite make up my mind between cookies, candy, or cheesecake . . . it doesn't matter! With this one, I don't have to choose!

1 package (18 ounces) refrigerated oatmeal cookie dough with chocolate and butterscotch chips (see Note)
2 packages (8 ounces each) cream cheese, softened
2 eggs
½ cup sugar
1 teaspoon vanilla extract
4 Heath® candy bars (1.4 ounces each), coarsely chopped

Preheat the oven to 350°F. Slice the cookie dough into 24 slices and arrange on the bottom and up the sides of a 9-inch deep-dish pie plate that has been coated with nonstick baking spray. Press the dough together, making a uniform crust; set aside. In a large bowl, with an electric beater on medium speed, beat the cream cheese, eggs, sugar, and vanilla for 1 minute, or until well mixed. Stir in the candy pieces and pour into the pie plate. Bake for 40 to 45 minutes, until the center is firm. Remove from the oven and allow to cool. Cover loosely, then chill for at least 4 hours, or overnight.

NOTE: To make the cookie dough easier to slice, freeze it for 2 to 3 hours before starting this recipe.

Snack-a-Snickers® Cheesecake

8 servings

When I was a kid, I loved to run down to the candy store and get a quick pick-me-up. So why not have that "feel like a kid" taste in my baked goods now? Yeah, why not?!

4 Snickers® candy bars (2.07 ounces each), coarsely chopped, divided
One 9-inch graham cracker pie crust
2 packages (8 ounces each) cream cheese, softened
½ cup sugar
2 eggs
1 teaspoon vanilla extract
¼ cup frozen whipped topping, thawed

Preheat the oven to 375°F. Spread ½ cup chopped candy in the bottom of the pie crust; set aside. In a large bowl, with an electric beater on medium speed, beat the cream cheese and sugar for 2 minutes, or until creamy. Add the eggs and vanilla and continue beating until thoroughly combined. Reserve 8 pieces of the candy for garnish and stir the remaining chopped candy into the cream cheese mixture; mix well. Pour into the crust and bake for 30 to 35 minutes, until almost set in the center. Remove from the oven and let cool for 15 to 20 minutes. Chill for at least 4 hours, or overnight. Garnish with the whipped topping and the reserved candy pieces and serve; or cover loosely and keep chilled until ready to serve.

NOTE: You can try almost any favorite candy bar in this cheesecake—maybe try a new one every time you make it!

Italian Meringue Cheesecake

8 to 10 servings

Fasten your aprons—we're taking a trip to Italy. Mamma mia! Feather-light meringue makes this one the tops.

1¾ cups all-purpose flour
¾ cup granulated sugar, divided
½ cup (1 stick) butter, melted
4 eggs
4 teaspoons grated orange rind, divided

½ teaspoon salt
1 container (2 pounds) ricotta cheese
1½ cups confectioners' sugar
¼ teaspoon ground cinnamon
3 egg whites

Preheat the oven to 375°F. In a medium-sized bowl, combine the flour, ½ cup granulated sugar, the melted butter, 2 eggs, 1 teaspoon orange rind, and the salt. Stir the mixture until it forms a ball, then place the dough in a 9-inch deep-dish pie plate. With your fingers, spread the dough into a smooth crust to cover the bottom and sides of the plate; chill while you prepare the filling. In a medium-sized bowl, with an electric beater on medium speed, beat the ricotta cheese, confectioners' sugar, the remaining 2 eggs and 1 tablespoon orange rind, and the cinnamon for 2 to 3 minutes, until well blended. Pour into the chilled crust and bake for 40 to 45 minutes, until almost set in the center. In a large bowl, with an electric beater on high speed, beat the egg whites and the remaining ¼ cup granulated sugar until stiff peaks form. Spread over the top of the pie, sealing the edges of the crust with the meringue. Bake for 15 to 20 minutes, until golden brown on top. Allow to cool to room temperature, then cover loosely and chill for at least 4 hours before serving.

Low-Fat Strawberry Cheesecake

8 to 10 servings

The next time the gang tells you they're coming over, ask if they'd rather have a low-fat dessert or cheesecake. Of course, with this one you get the best of both, slice after slice!

1 container (16 ounces) 1% low-fat cottage cheese
¾ cup egg substitute
4 ounces reduced-fat cream cheese, softened
⅓ cup plus 1 tablespoon sugar, divided

1 teaspoon vanilla extract
½ cup low-fat vanilla yogurt
⅛ teaspoon lemon juice
1 pint fresh strawberries, sliced

Preheat the oven to 350°F. In a blender, combine the cottage cheese, egg substitute, cream cheese, ⅓ cup sugar, and the vanilla. Cover and blend for 1 minute, or until smooth. Pour into a 9-inch pie plate that has been coated with nonstick baking spray. Bake for 35 to 40 minutes, until the center is firm. In a small bowl, combine the yogurt, the remaining 1 tablespoon sugar, and the lemon juice; mix well. Spread evenly over the cheesecake, then bake for 5 minutes. Remove from the oven and cool completely. Top with the sliced strawberries, then cover loosely and chill for at least 3 hours before serving.

NOTE: Sometimes I top this with a combination of raspberries, blackberries, and blueberries—or even sliced kiwifruit!

Cookies 'n' Cream Cheesecake

12 servings

Warning—this is one type of cookie that does *not* go in the cookie jar. But it sure is at home in the fridge . . . if it makes it that far!

1 package (20 ounces) cream-filled
   chocolate sandwich cookies
6 tablespoons butter, melted
3 packages (8 ounces each)
   cream cheese, softened
1¼ cups sugar, divided

4 eggs
2 teaspoons vanilla extract, divided
1 container (16 ounces) sour cream
1 tablespoon unsweetened cocoa
½ cup frozen whipped topping,
   thawed

Preheat the oven to 350°F. Place 30 cookies in a resealable plastic bag and finely crush, using a rolling pin. Place in a medium-sized bowl and add the butter; mix well. Spread over the bottom of a 10-inch springform pan. Chill until ready to use. In a large bowl, with an electric beater on medium speed, beat the cream cheese and 1 cup sugar until creamy. Add the eggs one at a time, beating well after each addition, then add 1 teaspoon vanilla; mix well. Set aside 6 of the remaining cookies for garnish, then break up the rest into large chunks and stir into the cream cheese mixture; pour into the pan. Bake for 55 to 60 minutes, until firm. Remove from the oven and let cool for 5 minutes. Meanwhile, in a medium-sized bowl, stir together the sour cream, cocoa, and the remaining ¼ cup sugar and 1 teaspoon vanilla until well mixed. Carefully spread over the top of the cheesecake and bake for 5 minutes. Let cool, then cover loosely and chill for at least 8 hours, or overnight. Remove the side of the springform pan and place the cake on a serving plate. Spoon 12 dollops of whipped topping evenly around the edge of the top of the cake. Cut each reserved cookie in half and place half a cookie on each dollop of whipped topping.

NOTE: During different holiday seasons, you can usually find sandwich cookies filled with colored creams. These make really festive cheesecakes!

No-Bake Eggnog Cheesecake

9 servings

Save this recipe for the holidays, 'cause when your oven is full of roasting turkey or glazed ham and all the trimmings, it's nice to know you can make a cheesecake that doesn't need any baking!

¾ cup graham cracker crumbs
½ cup sugar, divided
½ teaspoon ground nutmeg
¼ cup (½ stick) butter, melted
1 envelope (0.25 ounce) unflavored gelatin

¼ cup cold water
1 package (8 ounces) cream cheese, softened
1 cup eggnog
1 cup (½ pint) heavy cream

In a small bowl, combine the graham cracker crumbs, ¼ cup sugar, the nutmeg, and butter; mix well. Press into the bottom of an 8-inch square baking dish; set aside. In a small saucepan, combine the gelatin and water; set aside for 5 minutes to soften, then stir over low heat for 3 to 4 minutes, until the gelatin is dissolved. Remove from the heat; set aside. In a large bowl, with an electric beater on medium speed, beat the cream cheese and the remaining ¼ cup sugar until well blended. Stir in the dissolved gelatin and the eggnog until well blended. Refrigerate for 8 to 10 minutes, until slightly thickened. In a medium-sized bowl, whip the cream until stiff peaks form. Fold the whipped cream into the eggnog mixture, then pour over the prepared crust, cover, and chill for at least 3 hours before serving.

NOTE: For an extra-special holiday look, sprinkle the top with some additional nutmeg.

79

Chocolate Cherry Cheesecake

8 to 10 servings

If you like ooey, gooey chocolate-covered cherries, grab a fork and a tall glass of ice-cold milk, 'cause it's time for some of that richness right now!

2 packages (8 ounces each) cream cheese, softened
½ cup sugar
2 eggs
1 teaspoon vanilla extract
1 jar (10 ounces) maraschino cherries, well drained

½ cup (3 ounces) semisweet chocolate chips
One 9-inch graham cracker pie crust
1 container (8 ounces) frozen whipped topping, thawed
¼ teaspoon unsweetened cocoa

Preheat the oven to 375°F. In a large bowl, with an electric beater on medium speed, beat the cream cheese and sugar until creamy. Add the eggs and vanilla and continue beating until thoroughly combined. Set aside 8 cherries for garnish, then coarsely chop the rest. Add the chopped cherries and chocolate chips to the cream cheese mixture and mix well, then pour the mixture into the pie crust. Bake for 35 to 40 minutes, until the center is firm. Chill for 1 hour, then spread on the whipped topping and sprinkle with the cocoa powder. Garnish with the reserved cherries. Cover loosely and chill until ready to serve.

Chocolate Cheesecakes

two 9-inch cheesecakes, 8 to 10 servings each

I like to make two of these 'cause no self-respecting chocoholic can have just one! (And you know that everybody will be asking for "Seconds, please!")

3 packages (8 ounces each)
   cream cheese, softened
1 cup sugar
2 eggs
1 cup (6 ounces) semisweet
   chocolate chips, melted

¾ cup sour cream
½ cup cold black coffee
Two 9-inch graham cracker pie crusts

Preheat the oven to 350°F. In a medium-sized bowl, with an electric beater on medium speed, beat the cream cheese, sugar, and eggs until creamy. Add the melted chocolate, sour cream, and coffee. Continue beating until the mixture is smooth and uniform in color. Divide the mixture evenly between the pie crusts; bake for 1 hour, or until the centers are set. Turn off the oven and leave the cheesecakes in the oven with the door ajar for 1 hour. Allow to cool completely, then cover and chill for at least 2 hours before serving.

NOTE: Decorate as desired with whipped cream, cocoa, shaved chocolate, or any of your favorites. And, of course, you can freeze one of the cakes if you'd like. Just be sure to wrap it tightly in plastic wrap.

Tutti-Fruity Tarts

1 dozen tarts

Tickle the fancy of fruit fans everywhere with a taste of these tangy tarts.

2 packages (8 ounces each) cream cheese, softened
¼ cup orange marmalade
⅔ cup sugar

12 single-serving graham cracker tart shells
1 can (21 ounces) blueberry pie filling or topping (see Note)

In a medium-sized bowl, with an electric beater on medium speed, beat the cream cheese, marmalade, and sugar for 2 minutes, or until well combined. Spoon the mixture evenly into the tart shells, then top with the blueberry pie filling. Cover loosely and chill for at least 2 hours before serving.

NOTE: Top these with either blueberry or your favorite flavor of fruit topping, like cherry, pineapple, strawberry, or apple. You can even use a few flavors and top a few tarts with each flavor for a colorful assortment!

Chocolate Chip Cheesecake Cups

2 dozen cups

"Awesome!" "The best!" These are just a few of the rave reviews these got from my grandchildren. They just loved getting their very own cheesecakes!

1 package (18 ounces) refrigerated chocolate chip cookie dough
1 package (8 ounces) cream cheese, softened
⅓ cup sugar
½ teaspoon vanilla extract
About ½ teaspoon unsweetened cocoa

Preheat the oven to 375°F. Slice the cookie dough into 24 slices. Roll each slice into a ball and place the balls in 24 mini muffin cups that have been coated with nonstick baking spray. Press down the center of each, making a deep well. Bake for 10 to 12 minutes, or until the edges are set and the "crusts" are light brown. Remove from the oven and press down the center of each with a spoon, making an indentation. Let stand for 5 minutes, then remove to wire racks to cool completely. In a small bowl, with an electric beater on medium speed, beat the cream cheese, sugar, and vanilla until smooth. Spoon 1 teaspoon of the cream cheese mixture into each cup. Dust the tops with cocoa. Serve immediately, or cover and chill until ready to serve.

NOTE: Instead of dusting these with the cocoa, you might want to top them with some cherry pie filling for a cherry-chocolate mini-treat that kids of any age will love!

Peppermint Twist Cheesecakes

18 mini cheesecakes

I bet you'll like doing *this* twist. I mean, who wouldn't love bite-sized cheesecake morsels with minty candy dancing inside?!

18 chocolate wafer cookies
3 packages (8 ounces each)
    cream cheese, softened
2 eggs

½ cup confectioners' sugar
1 cup crushed candy canes or
    peppermint candies

Preheat the oven to 350°F. Line 18 regular-sized muffin cups with paper baking cups. Place a chocolate wafer in the bottom of each paper cup. In a large bowl, with an electric beater on medium speed, beat the cream cheese, eggs, and confectioners' sugar until creamy. Stir in the crushed candy. Spoon evenly into the paper cups and bake for 22 to 25 minutes, until set. Cool completely, then cover loosely and chill for at least 2 hours before serving.

NOTE: Top each cheesecake with whipped topping and a whole miniature candy cane for that perfect holiday treat.

Crustless Cheesecake Pie

8 to 10 servings

I shared this recipe on one of my early Mr. Food TV shows and all these years later, I'm still getting requests for it. I guess that means it can be considered a classic! I promise you'll be glad you made it.

2 packages (8 ounces each) cream cheese, softened
⅔ cup plus 3 tablespoons sugar, divided
3 eggs

1½ teaspoons vanilla extract, divided
½ teaspoon fresh lemon juice, divided
1 container (16 ounces) sour cream

Preheat the oven to 350°F. In a large bowl, with an electric beater on medium speed, beat the cream cheese and ⅔ cup sugar until smooth. Beat in the eggs one at a time, then beat in ½ teaspoon vanilla and ¼ teaspoon lemon juice. Pour into a 9-inch deep-dish glass pie plate that has been coated with nonstick baking spray. Bake for about 50 minutes, until golden. Remove from the oven and let cool for 15 minutes. Do not turn off the oven. In a medium-sized bowl, combine the sour cream and the remaining 3 tablespoons sugar, 1 teaspoon vanilla, and ¼ teaspoon lemon juice; mix well. Spread over the top of the pie and bake for 10 minutes; the top will still appear very wet. Let cool, then chill for at least 4 hours, or overnight.

NOTE: This tastes great just the way it is, but if you want, go ahead and cover it with pie filling or fresh berries before serving.

Pies

Chocolate–Peanut Butter Cream Pie

8 to 10 servings

All right, I admit it! I have a weakness for anything with chocolate and peanut butter. Actually, there are a lot of us who'll love the combination in this pie.

One 9-inch frozen ready-to-bake pie shell, thawed
1 package (4-serving size) cook-and-serve vanilla pudding and pie filling

2 cups milk
½ cup (3 ounces) semisweet chocolate chips
½ cup (3 ounces) peanut butter chips

Bake the pie shell according to the package directions; let cool. In a medium-sized saucepan, combine the pudding mix and milk over medium heat. Stir constantly until boiling, then remove from the heat. Pour half of the pudding into a small bowl. Add the chocolate chips to the bowl and stir until the chips are completely melted. Pour into the pie crust. Add the peanut butter chips to the remaining pudding and stir until the chips are completely melted. Carefully pour the peanut butter mixture over the chocolate mixture in the pie shell. Cover and chill for at least 4 hours, or until thoroughly chilled and set.

NOTE: Dress it up by spreading or dolloping the top of the pie with some whipped topping, then garnishing with miniature peanut butter cups.

Cappuccino Custard Pie

8 to 10 servings

Cappuccino is one of the trendiest coffee drinks, and for good reason! So why not enjoy that same flavor in a melt-in-your-mouth creamy pie?

6 eggs
¾ cup sugar
1 teaspoon vanilla extract

¼ teaspoon salt
4 cups (1 quart) half-and-half
2 tablespoons instant coffee granules

Preheat the oven to 325°F. In a large bowl, lightly beat the eggs, sugar, vanilla, and salt; set aside. In a medium-sized saucepan, heat the half-and-half and coffee granules over medium-low heat, stirring constantly, for 8 to 10 minutes, until the mixture is hot and the coffee is dissolved. Gradually beat the coffee mixture into the eggs until thoroughly mixed. Pour into a 9-inch deep-dish pie plate and place in a large shallow pan. Pour water into the pan to come about halfway up the sides of the pie plate, being careful not to pour any water into the pie plate. Bake for 60 to 65 minutes, until a knife inserted in the center comes out clean. Carefully remove the pie plate from the water and allow the pie to cool for 20 minutes. Chill for 1 hour, then cover and chill for at least 2 hours before serving.

NOTE: For a true cappuccino confection, garnish this with whipped cream and a dusting of cocoa powder.

Fresh Strawberry Pie

6 to 8 servings

Fresh from the berry patch, this pie is the perfect after-dinner treat for any time you want a taste of summer.

One 9-inch frozen ready-to-bake
   deep-dish pie shell, thawed
4 pints fresh strawberries, hulled
¾ cup sugar

3 tablespoons cornstarch
½ cup water
⅛ teaspoon red food color

Bake the pie shell according to the package directions; let cool. In a medium-sized saucepan, combine 1 pint strawberries with the sugar and cook over medium heat, crushing the strawberries with the back of a spoon, until the mixture is thickened and syrupy. In a small bowl, whisk together the cornstarch and water until the cornstarch is dissolved, then add to the strawberry mixture. Cook for 5 to 6 minutes, or until the mixture has thickened, stirring frequently. Remove from the heat, add the food color, and mix until well blended; allow to cool completely, then place in a large bowl. Add the remaining whole strawberries and mix until the strawberries are well coated. Spoon into the pie shell, cover loosely, and chill for at least 2 hours before serving.

NOTE: Wanna make them really go crazy? Top your pie slices with dollops of freshly whipped cream.

Peachy-Keen Cream Pie

8 to 10 servings

There's no other way to say it—this pie is peachy-keen through and through!

¾ cup firmly packed light brown sugar

¼ cup all-purpose flour

¼ teaspoon ground cinnamon

¼ teaspoon salt

1 cup (½ pint) heavy cream

1 can (29 ounces) sliced peaches, drained

One 9-inch frozen ready-to-bake deep-dish pie shell, thawed

Preheat the oven to 425°F. In a medium-sized bowl, combine the brown sugar, flour, cinnamon, and salt. Add the cream; mix well. Place the peaches in the pie shell and pour the cream mixture over them. Bake for 35 to 40 minutes, until firm in the center. Remove from the oven and let cool for 20 to 30 minutes. Chill for at least 2 hours; serve, or cover and keep chilled until ready to serve.

NOTE: Serve with a scoop of vanilla ice cream for an extra-creamy Peachy-Keen Cream Pie.

Pineapple Pistachio Pie

8 to 10 servings

Looking for something to serve that's a little out of the ordinary? Chances are, you won't find *this* one at the bakery!

2 cups shortbread cookie crumbs
¾ cup chopped walnuts, divided
¼ cup (½ stick) butter, melted
1 package (8 ounces) cream cheese, softened
1 can (14 ounces) sweetened condensed milk

¼ cup lime juice
1 package (4-serving size) instant pistachio pudding and pie filling
1 can (8 ounces) crushed pineapple, undrained
1 cup (½ pint) heavy cream

Preheat the oven to 350°F. In a medium-sized bowl, combine the cookie crumbs, ¼ cup walnuts, and the butter. Press into the bottom and up the sides of a 9-inch deep-dish pie plate to form a crust. Bake for 10 minutes, then remove from the oven and allow to cool. Meanwhile, in a large bowl, with an electric beater on medium speed, beat the cream cheese for about 1 minute, until fluffy. Add the sweetened condensed milk, lime juice, and pudding mix and continue beating for 2 to 3 minutes, until smooth. Stir in the remaining ½ cup walnuts and the pineapple. In a medium-sized bowl, with an electric beater on medium speed, beat the cream until stiff peaks form. Fold the whipped cream into the pudding mixture and pour into the pie crust. Cover and chill for at least 6 hours, or overnight.

NOTE: Any type of shortbread cookies can be crumbled to create the cookie crumbs—even cookies that have nuts in them. But if you use cookies with nuts, leave out the ¼ cup of walnuts that go into this crust.

Fruit Medley Pie

10 to 12 servings

When you want to please everybody "for a song," bring out this creamy, fruity treat. The applause will be music to your ears!

1¾ cups plus 2 tablespoons graham cracker crumbs, divided
3 tablespoons sugar
½ cup (1 stick) butter, melted
2 packages (4 servings each) instant banana cream pudding and pie filling
3 cups cold milk
1 container (12 ounces) frozen whipped topping, thawed

1 banana, peeled and sliced
1 pint fresh strawberries, hulled
1 kiwifruit, peeled and cut into ¼-inch-thick slices
½ pint fresh blueberries
1 orange, peeled and cut into ¼-inch-thick slices
¼ cup apple jelly, melted

Preheat the oven to 350°F. In a medium-sized bowl, combine 1¾ cups graham cracker crumbs, the sugar, and butter until well mixed. Press into the bottom and up the sides of a 9-inch deep-dish pie plate, forming a crust. Bake for 8 minutes; let cool completely. In a medium-sized bowl, whisk the pudding mixes and milk until well combined and thickened. Pour into the cooled pie shell. Top with the whipped topping, mounding it in the center and tapering down to the crust. Sprinkle with the remaining 2 tablespoons graham cracker crumbs. Arrange the banana, strawberries, kiwi, blueberries, and orange slices over the top of the pie as illustrated. Using a pastry brush, brush the fruit with the melted jelly. Cover loosely and chill for at least 4 hours before serving.

NOTE: Here's just one way you can arrange the fruit. How you do it is up to you. You can even include more or less fresh fruit, depending on what you have on hand.

Best Ambrosia Pie

8 to 10 servings

For centuries, *ambrosia* has meant "the best," . . . and this pie is no exception!

1 package (7 ounces) flaked coconut, toasted (see Note, page 6)
⅓ cup butter, melted
1 can (14 ounces) sweetened condensed milk
⅓ cup lemon juice

1 can (16 ounces) fruit cocktail, well drained
1 cup miniature marshmallows
2 cups frozen whipped topping, thawed

Reserve 2 tablespoons coconut for garnish. In a small bowl, combine the remaining coconut and the butter; mix well. Spread into a 9-inch deep-dish pie plate that has been coated with nonstick baking spray, pressing firmly into the bottom and up the sides of the plate to form a crust. Place in the refrigerator to chill. In a large bowl, combine the sweetened condensed milk, lemon juice, fruit cocktail, and marshmallows. Stir gently until well mixed. Fold in the whipped topping, then spoon into the prepared crust. Garnish with the reserved coconut, then cover and chill for at least 4 hours, or until set.

NOTE: Top with maraschino cherries or mandarin orange segments for an extra burst of color.

96

Pine-Apple Pie

6 to 8 servings

Have this pie ready and waiting for your family, and you're sure to be the "apple" of their eyes!

One 9-inch frozen ready-to-bake deep-dish pie shell, thawed
1½ cups pineapple juice, divided
1 can (8 ounces) crushed pineapple, undrained
¾ cup sugar

5 large apples, cored, peeled, and cut into wedges
3 tablespoons cornstarch
1 tablespoon butter
½ teaspoon vanilla extract
¼ teaspoon salt

Bake the pie shell according to the package directions; let cool. In a large saucepan, combine 1¼ cups pineapple juice, the crushed pineapple with its juice, and the sugar. Bring to a boil over medium-high heat, then add the apples and return to a boil. Reduce the heat to medium, cover, and cook for 5 to 7 minutes, or until the apples are tender. Using a slotted spoon, remove the apples to a bowl; set aside. In a small bowl, dissolve the cornstarch in the remaining ¼ cup pineapple juice. Add to the saucepan and cook over low heat for about 1 minute, until the pineapple mixture has thickened. Remove from the heat and add the butter, vanilla, and salt, mixing well. Return the apples to the saucepan and gently stir until evenly coated. Spoon into the pie crust and chill for at least 3 hours; serve, or cover loosely and keep chilled until ready to serve.

NOTE: Cortland and Granny Smith apples work especially well in this pie.

Kiwi Lime Pie

8 to 10 servings

With its tangy tartness and hint of sweetness, this is a real "sweet-tart" of a pie! (And covered with bright-green kiwi slices, it's an eye-catcher, for sure.)

One 9-inch frozen ready-to-bake
    pie shell, thawed
1 can (14 ounces) sweetened
    condensed milk
1 can (6 ounces) frozen limeade
    concentrate, thawed

1 container (8 ounces) frozen
    whipped topping, thawed
2 kiwifruit, peeled and thinly sliced

Bake the pie shell according to the package directions; let cool. In a large bowl, combine the sweetened condensed milk and limeade; mix well. Fold in the whipped topping. Spoon into the baked pie crust and chill for 4 hours, or until set. Top with the kiwi slices and serve, or cover and keep chilled until ready to serve.

NOTE: A few fresh raspberries sprinkled on top add a nice color contrast.

Lemon Crunch Pie

8 to 10 servings

Another run-of-the-mill lemon pie? No way! Fruity lemon drops add crunch and pizzazz to make this a second-helping hit.

30 lemon-cream–filled vanilla
    sandwich cookies, finely crushed
¼ cup (½ stick) butter, melted
2 packages (4 servings each)
    instant lemon pudding and
    pie filling, prepared according to
    the package directions

1 container (8 ounces) frozen
    whipped topping, thawed
½ cup finely crushed lemon drop
    candies (see Note)

Preheat the oven to 350°F. In a medium-sized bowl, combine the crushed cookies and the butter; mix well. Spread over the bottom and up the sides of a 9-inch deep-dish pie plate, forming a crust. Bake for 10 minutes, then remove from the oven and allow to cool completely. Spoon the pudding evenly into the pie crust. In a large bowl, combine the whipped topping and crushed candy; mix well. Spread over the pie filling, then cover loosely and chill for at least 2 hours before serving.

NOTE: You can use a blender or a food processor to crush the lemon drops. And you can even put them in a resealable plastic storage bag, seal, and pound with a mallet! Make sure to crush the lemon drops to a very fine powder before mixing with the whipped topping. Otherwise, they'll weigh it down.

Berry Bavarian Pie

6 to 8 servings

This is a light, cool-ya-down dessert that's perfect for a hot summer day!

1 package (4-serving size)
   strawberry-flavored gelatin
1⅓ cups boiling water
Juice of 1 lemon
¼ cup seedless raspberry jam

1 container (8 ounces) frozen
   whipped topping, thawed
One 9-inch chocolate graham cracker
   pie crust

In a large bowl, combine the gelatin, water, and lemon juice; mix until the gelatin is dissolved. Cover and chill for about 2 hours, until slightly thickened but not set. Beat with an electric beater on medium speed for about 30 seconds, or until broken up. Add the raspberry jam and whipped topping and continue beating for 2 to 3 minutes, or until thoroughly combined. Pour into the pie crust, cover, and chill for at least 4 hours, or until firm.

NOTE: Top with additional whipped topping and fresh raspberries, if desired.

Pecan-Crusted Chocolate Pie

12 to 16 servings

A little goes a long way here, so invite the whole gang over to enjoy their favorite tastes—chocolate and crunchy pecans!

2 cups pecan halves, divided
⅓ cup sugar
¼ cup (½ stick) unsalted butter, melted

2 tablespoons caramel topping
1½ cups heavy cream
2 cups (12 ounces) semisweet chocolate chips

Preheat the oven to 350°F. In a food processor that has been fitted with its metal cutting blade or a blender, finely chop 1¾ cups pecans with the sugar. Add the butter and continue processing until completely blended. Press into the bottom and up the sides of a 9-inch pie plate, forming a crust. Bake for 20 to 25 minutes, or until browned. Remove from the oven and allow to cool. Drizzle the caramel topping over the crust. In a medium-sized saucepan, heat the cream over medium heat, until almost boiling. Reduce the heat to low and stir in the chocolate chips. Continue cooking until the chocolate melts and the mixture is smooth, whisking continuously. Remove from the heat and let cool to lukewarm, then pour into the pie crust. Garnish with the remaining ¼ cup pecan halves and chill for at least 2 hours before serving.

NOTE: This is an extra-rich pie, so a small slice goes a long way!

Dreamy Mocha Cream Pie

8 to 10 servings

Wanna create a sensation? Dazzle your guests with this dreamy no-bake cream pie. They won't believe you made it yourself!

One 9-inch ready-to-bake deep-dish
    pie shell, thawed
1 cup granulated sugar
⅓ cup unsweetened cocoa
⅓ cup cornstarch
¼ teaspoon salt
2¾ cups milk

2 tablespoons plus 1 teaspoon
    coffee-flavored liqueur, divided
1 tablespoon butter
1 teaspoon vanilla extract
1 cup (½ pint) heavy cream
2 tablespoons confectioners' sugar

Bake the pie shell according to the package directions; let cool. Meanwhile, in a medium-sized saucepan, combine the granulated sugar, cocoa, cornstarch, and salt. Gradually blend in the milk and cook over medium heat for 6 to 8 minutes, until the mixture comes to a boil, stirring constantly. Remove from the heat and stir in 2 tablespoons coffee liqueur, the butter, and vanilla until well blended. Pour into the cooled pie crust and chill for 1 hour. In a small bowl, with an electric beater on medium speed, combine the heavy cream and confectioners' sugar and beat until soft peaks form. Add the remaining 1 teaspoon coffee liqueur and continue beating until stiff peaks form. Spread over the pie, cover loosely, and chill for at least 5 hours before serving.

NOTE: For a really fancy touch, top with shaved chocolate or chocolate curls.

Peanut Butter Cup Pie

8 servings

All it takes to have a winner is a good team—and what better duo than peanut butter and chocolate for the perfect finish to any meal?!

1 container (12 ounces) frozen whipped topping, thawed
1½ cups creamy peanut butter (see Note)

16 miniature peanut butter cups
1½ teaspoons vanilla extract
One 9-inch chocolate graham cracker pie crust

In a large bowl, combine the whipped topping and peanut butter; mix until thoroughly combined and set aside. With a knife, cut 12 peanut butter cups into quarters. Fold the quartered peanut butter cups and the vanilla into the whipped topping mixture, then spoon into the crust. Cut the remaining 4 peanut butter cups into halves and use to garnish the top of the pie. Cover and chill for at least 2 hours before serving.

NOTE: For lovers of extra crunch, sure, it's fine to use crunchy-style peanut butter.

Easy Key Lime Pie

8 to 10 servings

So you thought you'd have to travel to the Florida Keys to find this regional specialty? Not anymore! Now you have the secret to whipping it up right at home.

3 egg yolks
1½ teaspoons grated lime peel
1 can (14 ounces) sweetened
   condensed milk

⅔ cup Key lime juice (see Note)
One 9-inch graham cracker pie crust

Preheat the oven to 350°F. In a medium-sized bowl, with an electric beater on medium speed, beat the egg yolks and grated lime peel for 5 minutes, or until fluffy. Gradually add the sweetened condensed milk and continue beating for 4 minutes. Reduce the speed to low and gradually beat in the lime juice just until combined. Pour the filling into the pie crust and bake for about 10 minutes, until firm in the center. Remove from the oven and let cool on a wire rack, then cover and chill for at least 2 hours before serving. This is best served very cold, so freeze it for 15 to 20 minutes before serving.

NOTE: Go ahead and top this with whipped cream or whipped topping and garnish with fresh lime slices, if desired. If you can't find Key limes or Key lime juice, it's okay to substitute regular lime juice—the pie just won't be as tart.

Frozen Desserts

Block Party Ice Cream Cake

12 to 16 servings

The best way to spread smiles around the neighborhood is to have a really "cool" block party. And this recipe takes the cake!

1 block (½ gallon) vanilla fudge swirl ice cream
1 container (8 ounces) frozen whipped topping, thawed

1 jar (12 ounces) hot fudge sauce
1 package (3 ounces) ladyfingers, split in half

Remove the block of ice cream from the package and place on a serving platter, then spread the whipped topping evenly around the sides of the block. Spread the fudge sauce over the top of the block, then place the ladyfingers standing up against the whipped topping so that they line the outside of the block of ice cream (see illustration). Freeze for at least 1 hour, or until firm, then serve, or cover and keep frozen until ready to serve.

NOTE: This is the perfect cake for any party—just use a tube of decorating gel to personalize a greeting in the fudge sauce.

I'm a chip off the old block!

Pineapple Freezer Cake

8 to 10 servings

When it's hot out and we don't want to turn on the oven, how do we bake a special cake? We pop it in the freezer!

2 packages (3 ounces each) ladyfingers, split in half (see Note)
1 can (20 ounces) crushed pineapple, drained

1 package (6-serving size) instant vanilla pudding and pie filling
1 container (16 ounces) frozen whipped topping, thawed

Line a 9" × 5" loaf pan with plastic wrap. Line the bottom and sides of the pan with a layer of ladyfingers. In a large bowl, combine the pineapple and pudding mix; mix well, then fold in the whipped topping. Spread one quarter of the mixture over the bottom layer of ladyfingers, then repeat the layers 3 more times, ending with a layer of pudding mixture. Cover and freeze for at least 2 hours, or overnight. To serve, invert onto a serving platter, remove the pan and plastic wrap, and cut into slices.

NOTE: Make sure to use the soft, spongy ladyfingers, not the hard biscuit type.

Cherry Ice Cream Cake

12 to 16 servings

Don't "freeze up" when you find out company's coming. Make this the night before—it takes no time to put together, the freezer does all the work, and you look like a kitchen hero!

1 quart chocolate ice cream, slightly softened
1½ cups crushed chocolate wafer cookies (about 24 cookies)
1 can (17 ounces) pitted dark cherries, drained and patted dry

1 quart strawberry ice cream, slightly softened
1 quart vanilla ice cream, slightly softened

Spread the chocolate ice cream to cover the bottom of a 10-inch springform pan. Sprinkle with ½ cup crushed cookies. Place the cherries evenly over the cookies, then cover completely with the strawberry ice cream. Sprinkle another ½ cup crushed cookies over the strawberry ice cream, then top with the vanilla ice cream, covering completely. Sprinkle the remaining ½ cup crushed cookies over the top, cover, and freeze for 3 to 4 hours, or overnight. When ready to serve, remove the springform ring and allow the cake to stand for 10 minutes before slicing into wedges.

NOTE: Make sure that after serving you get any remaining cake covered and right back into the freezer!

Raspberry 'n' Cream Brownies

10 to 12 servings

With its cooling raspberry and vanilla layered between rich, chewy brownie wedges, this one'll give you one heavenly bite after another!

1 package (22.5 ounces) brownie
   mix, batter prepared according
   to the package directions
1 quart vanilla ice cream, softened

1 quart raspberry sherbet, softened
2 cups (1 pint) heavy cream
3 tablespoons confectioners' sugar
½ teaspoon vanilla extract

Preheat the oven to 350°F. Coat a 10" × 15" rimmed baking sheet with nonstick baking spray, line it with waxed paper, and coat the waxed paper with nonstick baking spray. Spoon the brownie batter onto the prepared baking sheet. Bake for 20 to 25 minutes, or until a wooden toothpick inserted in the center comes out clean; allow to cool. Remove the brownie from the baking sheet and carefully remove the waxed paper. Cut crosswise into 3 equal sections (each measuring 10" × 5"). Place 1 section on a serving platter and spread the vanilla ice cream over the top, covering it completely. Place the second brownie section over the ice cream and press down gently with the back of the baking sheet. Cover completely with the raspberry sherbet, then top with the third brownie section, again pressing down with the baking sheet. Cover with plastic wrap and freeze for 2 to 3 hours, until frozen. In a medium-sized bowl, with an electric beater on medium speed, beat the cream, confectioners' sugar, and vanilla until stiff peaks form. Remove the brownie cake from the freezer and frost the top and sides with the whipped cream. Return to the freezer for 1 to 2 hours, then cover and keep frozen until ready to serve. Remove from the freezer 10 minutes before serving.

NOTE: This will keep in the freezer for several days.

Belgian Chocolate Pie

8 to 10 servings

Belgian chocolate pie without Belgian chocolate? Sure! With our secret ingredient, we can create the taste without the expense.

1 teaspoon instant coffee granules
2 teaspoons hot water
1 can (14 ounces) sweetened
  condensed milk
1 cup (6 ounces) semisweet
  chocolate chips, melted

1 cup (½ pint) heavy cream
One 9-inch chocolate graham cracker
  pie crust

In a large bowl, dissolve the coffee granules in the hot water. Add the sweetened condensed milk and melted chocolate, stirring until smooth. Chill for 10 minutes. In a medium-sized bowl, with an electric beater on high speed, beat the cream until stiff peaks form. Fold the whipped cream into the chocolate mixture, then pour into the pie crust. Cover and freeze for at least 6 hours, until firm.

NOTE: Give this a fancy look by topping it with some whipped cream dollops and chocolate-covered coffee beans.

Caramel Peanut Brittle Pie

8 to 10 servings

"How'd ya do it?" "I have to have the recipe!" Tell 'em it's a secret—'cause they'll never figure out how easy it was to throw together!

1 pint vanilla ice cream, softened
1 cup coarsely crushed peanut brittle
  (see Note)
½ cup coarsely crushed graham
  crackers

½ cup caramel sauce
One 9-inch graham cracker pie crust

In a large bowl, combine the ice cream, peanut brittle, and crushed graham crackers; stir until well combined. Swirl in the caramel sauce, then spoon the mixture into the pie crust. Cover and freeze for at least 4 hours before serving.

NOTE: Almond toffee brittle or any type of brittle can be used, but don't crush it too fine.

Frozen Turtle Pie

12 to 14 servings

There's no reason we can't have a little fun with our food now and then. Cute little "turtles" are peeking out from all over this delightful dessert.

1 package (16 ounces) pecan
  shortbread cookies, coarsely
  crushed
1 jar (12.25 ounces) caramel sauce

½ gallon chocolate ice cream
1½ cups pecan halves, toasted
  (see Note, page 6)

In a large bowl, combine the crushed cookies and caramel sauce; mix well. Place half of the mixture in the bottom of a 9-inch deep-dish pie plate. Using half the ice cream, place individual scoops of ice cream over the cookie mixture. Place 2 pecan halves in the front and 2 pecan halves in the back of each scoop of ice cream, making "legs," and place 1 pecan half on top, making the "head" of a turtle (see illustration). Sprinkle with one quarter of the remaining cookie mixture, then top with more scoops of ice cream and

pecans, continuing in a pyramid shape until all the ingredients are used (see illustration). Cover and freeze for at least 3 hours before serving.

NOTE: I like the flavor of chocolate ice cream in this pie but, as usual, any flavor will do.

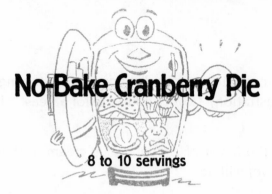

No-Bake Cranberry Pie

8 to 10 servings

Any way you slice it, this pie's a breeze to make. And the best part about it? It's another no-bake!

1½ cups graham cracker crumbs
3 tablespoons granulated sugar
½ cup (1 stick) butter, melted
1 package (8 ounces) cream cheese, softened
1 can (16 ounces) whole berry cranberry sauce (see Note)

1 can (8 ounces) crushed pineapple, drained and squeezed dry
½ cup chopped walnuts
1 cup sour cream
2 tablespoons light brown sugar

In a medium-sized bowl, combine the graham cracker crumbs, granulated sugar, and butter. Press into the bottom and up the sides of a 9-inch deep-dish pie plate, forming a crust. In a medium-sized bowl, with an electric beater on low speed, beat the cream cheese, cranberry sauce, pineapple, and walnuts until well combined, then spoon into the pie crust. In a small bowl, combine the sour cream and brown sugar. Spoon over the cranberry mixture, cover, and freeze for at least 4 hours, or overnight. Thaw for 5 minutes before slicing and serving.

NOTE: Whole berry cranberry sauce adds nice chunks of cranberries, but traditional cranberry sauce can also be used.

Lacy Ice Cream Pie

8 to 10 servings

The lacy chocolate topping gives this a crunch that'll win you over bite after bite.

1 container (7.25 ounces) chocolate-
  flavored hard-shell topping
  (see Note)

One 9-inch graham cracker pie crust
1 quart chocolate chip ice cream,
  softened

Pour half the hard-shell topping into the pie crust, and spread it carefully up the sides until the entire crust is coated. Spread half the ice cream over the hard-shell topping. Drizzle half the remaining hard-shell topping over the ice cream in a crisscross pattern. Repeat the layers, ending with the hard-shell topping. Cover loosely and freeze for at least 2 hours before serving.

NOTE: Hard-shell ice cream topping can usually be found with the other toppings and sauces in the ice cream or baking section of your supermarket.

Possible Pumpkin Pie

8 to 10 servings

This one's possible for anyone . . . even first-timers can whip it up in no time!

1 can (15 ounces) solid-pack pure pumpkin
1 can (14 ounces) sweetened condensed milk
1 teaspoon lemon juice
1 teaspoon ground cinnamon

½ teaspoon ground nutmeg
½ teaspoon salt
1 container (8 ounces) frozen whipped topping, thawed, divided
One 9-inch graham cracker pie crust

In a large bowl, with an electric beater on medium speed, beat the pumpkin, sweetened condensed milk, lemon juice, cinnamon, nutmeg, and salt until well blended. Add three quarters of the whipped topping and stir until smooth. Spoon into the pie crust, cover, and freeze for at least 6 hours, until firm. When ready to serve, dollop with the remaining whipped topping and slice into wedges.

NOTE: For extra color and flavor, sprinkle the dollops of whipped topping with some additional nutmeg.

Frozen Pecan Cheesecake

8 to 10 servings

This one's definitely worth the wait, 'cause after a few hours in the freezer, out pops one super sensation!

2 cups finely crushed shortbread cookies
2 cups chopped pecans, divided
½ cup (1 stick) butter, softened, divided
⅓ cup half-and-half

1 package (6 ounces) white baking bars
2 packages (8 ounces each) cream cheese, softened
⅓ cup confectioners' sugar
1 teaspoon vanilla extract

Preheat the oven to 350°F. In a medium-sized bowl, combine the crushed cookies, 1 cup pecans, and ¼ cup butter. Mix well and press into the bottom of a 9-inch deep-dish pie plate. Bake for 10 minutes, then remove from the oven and let cool. In a medium-sized saucepan, combine the half-and-half and white baking bars. Stir constantly over medium heat until the bars have melted and the mixture is smooth; remove from the heat and allow to cool slightly. In a medium-sized bowl, with an electric beater on medium speed, beat the cream cheese, confectioners' sugar, vanilla, and the remaining 1 cup nuts and ¼ cup butter for 3 to 4 minutes, until thoroughly blended. Add the half-and-half mixture, beating for 3 to 4 minutes, until thoroughly blended. Pour into the crust, cover, and freeze for at least 6 hours, or overnight. Remove from the freezer and allow to thaw for 15 minutes before serving.

119

Banana Split Bombe

16 to 20 servings

Ready to run down to the ice cream parlor and order up a fruit-filled sundae? Save your steps, 'cause you'll be "bowled over" by the shape this one's in.

½ gallon Neapolitan ice cream
1 jar (12 ounces) hot fudge sauce
2 medium-sized bananas, sliced

1 jar (12 ounces) pineapple preserves
2 cups frozen whipped topping, thawed

Divide the three flavors of ice cream and allow to soften slightly. Line a 3- to 4-quart bowl with plastic wrap. Spread the chocolate ice cream in the bottom of the bowl. Top with the fudge topping and half of the sliced bananas. Spread the strawberry ice cream over the bananas, then top with the pineapple preserves and the remaining sliced bananas. Spread the vanilla ice cream over the top, then cover and freeze for at least 4 hours, or overnight. Remove from the freezer and invert onto a serving platter. Remove the bowl and plastic wrap, then frost with the whipped topping. Return to the freezer for at least 1 hour, or until the topping has frozen. Serve, or cover and keep frozen until ready to serve.

NOTE: After slicing, top each serving with a maraschino cherry to give it a banana split finishing touch.

Chocolate Chip Dome

12 to 16 servings

Forget the cookie jar and head straight for the freezer. They'll flip for chilly chocolate chip wedges.

1½ cups milk
¾ cup coffee-flavored liqueur
1 package (18 ounces) chocolate
  chip cookies

1 container (16 ounces) frozen
  whipped topping, thawed

In a medium-sized bowl, combine the milk and liqueur. Line a 2-quart bowl with plastic wrap. Dip the chocolate chip cookies, a few at a time, into the milk mixture until moist, then use to line the bowl completely. Cover and refrigerate 1 cup of the whipped topping; cover the cookies with a ½-inch-thick layer of the remaining whipped topping. Repeat the layers until all the cookies are used, discarding any leftover milk mixture. Cover the bowl and freeze for at least 4 hours, or overnight. Remove from the freezer and invert onto a serving platter; remove the bowl and plastic wrap. Frost with the reserved whipped topping. Serve, or cover loosely and keep frozen; remove from the freezer and let stand for 10 minutes before cutting into pie-shaped wedges.

NOTE: Soak the chocolate chip cookies until they are soft but not falling apart. Make sure to use thin chocolate chip cookies, such as the Chips Ahoy® brand.

Pirate's Pound Cake

16 to 20 servings

"Yo ho ho and a bottle of rum . . . "?! If you've always dreamed of the excitement of a pirate's life, wait till you get a bite of this grown-up frozen fantasy.

1 pound cake (16 ounces), cut into 16 slices
½ cup light or dark rum, divided
1 container (16 ounces) frozen whipped topping, thawed

1 container (8 ounces) chopped mixed candied fruit
1 cup chopped pecans, divided

Place the pound cake slices on a cutting board and drizzle with ¼ cup rum. Place 1 cup of the whipped topping in a small bowl; cover and chill. In a medium-sized bowl, combine the remaining whipped topping and ¼ cup rum. Place half of the mixture in another medium-sized bowl and mix in the candied fruit. Mix ¾ cup pecans into the other half of the whipped topping mixture. Line a 3-quart mold or bowl with plastic wrap. Line the mold with 12 slices of cake. Spoon the fruit mixture into the mold, then top with the remaining 4 slices of cake. Top with the pecan mixture, then cover and freeze for at least 6 hours. Remove from the freezer and invert onto a serving platter; remove the mold and plastic wrap. Frost with the reserved 1 cup whipped topping and sprinkle with the remaining ¼ cup pecans; return to the freezer for at least 2 hours, or until the topping has frozen. Serve, or cover and keep frozen until ready to serve.

NOTE: Be sure to wrap any leftovers well in plastic wrap and keep frozen.

122

I-Scream Pizza

10 to 12 servings

You'll be screaming with delight when you realize this pizza is made of ice cream and, oh, boy—candy!

1 package (18 ounces) refrigerated
   sugar cookie dough
1 quart strawberry ice cream,
   softened

1 cup flaked coconut
1 cup malted milk balls

Preheat the oven to 350°F. Using your fingertips or the heel of your hand, spread the cookie dough over a 12-inch pizza pan. Bake on the center rack of the oven for 10 to 12 minutes, until golden. Remove from the oven and let cool completely. Spread the ice cream evenly over the cooled cookie crust and sprinkle with the coconut. Push the malted milk balls into the ice cream. Cover and freeze for at least 3 hours before serving.

NOTE: Topping a pizza is a personal matter, so, just as in traditional pizza, this pizza can be topped with malted milk balls or almost any of your favorite candy or ice cream toppings.

Chocolate Dream Ice Cream

8 to 10 servings

Dreams *can* come true—like a fancy dessert without a lot of fuss. You'd better believe it!

1 quart chocolate ice cream, softened
1 container (8 ounces) frozen
   whipped topping, thawed

1 container (7¼ ounces) chocolate-
   flavored hard-shell topping
   (see Note, page 117)

Line a 9" × 5" loaf pan with plastic wrap. In a medium-sized bowl, with an electric beater on medium speed, beat the ice cream and whipped topping for 30 to 45 seconds, until soft and well blended. Spoon one quarter of the ice cream mixture into the pan. Pour one fourth of the hard-shell topping over the ice cream and quickly spread with a pastry brush so that it covers the ice cream completely. Repeat the ice cream and topping layers 3 more times, ending with the topping. Cover tightly and freeze for 6 to 8 hours, until firm. When ready to serve, invert onto a serving platter, remove the pan and plastic wrap, and slice.

NOTE: The flavor combinations are endless for this Dream. Make a Mocha Dream with coffee ice cream and chocolate hard-shell topping. With chocolate ice cream and peanut-flavored hard-shell topping, you've got Peanut Butter Cup Dream . . . and on and on!

Frozen Novelties

Chocolate Pudding Pops

6 pops

When the gang's on the go, give 'em something creamy-delicious to go with 'em!

⅔ cup sugar
¼ cup unsweetened cocoa
3 tablespoons cornstarch
¼ teaspoon salt
2¼ cups milk

1 teaspoon vanilla extract

Six 5-ounce paper cups
6 nontoxic wooden craft sticks

In a medium-sized saucepan, combine the sugar, cocoa, cornstarch, and salt. Gradually stir in the milk. Bring to a boil over medium heat, stirring constantly. Remove from the heat and stir in the vanilla. Allow to cool slightly, then spoon into the paper cups. Place a wooden stick in the center of each and freeze overnight, or until solid. Serve, or cover each pop with plastic wrap and keep frozen until ready to serve.

NOTE: What's the best way to remove your pop from its cup? Simply peel the paper away, or place your hands around the cup to warm the sides so that the pop can be pulled out of the cup.

Frozen Piña Coladas

18 servings

Check these out—they've got the same taste we love in our tropical piña colada drinks, but these are spoonable, and we can serve them up right from the freezer.

1 container (12 ounces) frozen whipped topping, thawed
1 can (15 ounces) cream of coconut

1 can (8 ounces) crushed pineapple, well drained
½ cup flaked coconut

Line 18 regular-sized muffin cups with paper baking cups. In a large bowl, combine the whipped topping and cream of coconut until well blended. Add the crushed pineapple and the coconut. Spoon into the baking cups, cover, and freeze for at least 3 hours before serving.

NOTE: Go the extra step to make these real tropical-looking treats—sprinkle each one with toasted flaked coconut and top it with a cherry and a paper umbrella.

Peanut Sundae Cones

12 cones

These are just like the ones we remember waiting in line for at the neighborhood ice cream truck. And now there's no need to wait for that bell to ring—we can make these ourselves in a jiffy!

Twelve 5-ounce paper cups
1 cup chopped salted peanuts,
    divided
1 cup (6 ounces) semisweet
    chocolate chips

2 tablespoons vegetable shortening
1 quart vanilla ice cream
12 sugar cones

Place 1 teaspoon of the nuts in the bottom of each paper cup. In a medium-sized microwave-safe bowl, heat the chocolate and shortening in the microwave on high power for about 1 minute. Stir until smooth and completely melted; heat for additional 10-second intervals if necessary. Stir the remaining nuts into the melted chocolate. Place about 2 teaspoons of the mixture into each cup, enough to come halfway up the side of each cup. Place a scoop of ice cream in a cone and invert the cone into the cup, pressing the ice cream into the chocolate mixture. Repeat with the remaining cones. Freeze the cones (in the cups) for 3 to 4 hours. When ready to serve, just peel the paper off each ice cream cone.

Drop-in Ice Cream Sandwiches

12 sandwiches

There used to be a drugstore in downtown Troy where a bunch of us would stop after school for ice cream. Well, that drugstore is long gone, but I can still remember the fun we had munching our afternoon ice cream sandwich treats. It's easy to make these at home now, so why not treat yourself and your kids?!

1 package (16 ounces) cream-filled chocolate sandwich cookies, crushed (see Note)

⅓ cup butter, melted
½ gallon vanilla ice cream, slightly softened

Place the crushed cookies in a medium-sized bowl. Add the melted butter; mix well. Press half of the mixture firmly into the bottom of a foil-lined 9" × 13" baking pan. Spread the softened ice cream over the cookie mixture, then gently press the remaining cookie mixture over the ice cream. Cover and freeze for at least 6 hours. Cut into 12 squares and serve, or wrap each square individually and keep frozen for an always-ready dessert snack.

NOTE: You can crush the sandwich cookies in a food processor or by placing them in a resealable plastic storage bag and rolling a rolling pin over them.

Banana Split Cream Puffs

12 cream puffs

It's part cream puff, part ice cream sandwich, and *all* down-right yummy!

1 cup water
½ cup (1 stick) butter, cut into
    quarters
¼ teaspoon salt
1 cup all-purpose flour
4 eggs, at room temperature

2 large bananas, peeled and sliced
    into 18 slices each
½ gallon vanilla ice cream
¼ cup strawberry preserves
¾ cup hot fudge sauce

Preheat the oven to 400°F. In a medium-sized saucepan, bring the water, butter, and salt to a boil over high heat. Add the flour all at once and stir quickly with a wooden spoon until the mixture forms a ball. Remove from the heat. Add 1 egg to the mixture and beat hard with the wooden spoon to blend. Add the remaining eggs one at a time, beating well after each addition; each egg must be completely blended before the next egg is added. As you beat the mixture, it will change from looking almost curdled to smooth. When it becomes smooth, spoon out ¼ cup of the mixture for each of 12 pastry puffs, spacing the puffs evenly on a large ungreased cookie sheet. Bake for 30 to 35 minutes, until golden and puffed; cool on a wire rack. Cut each pastry puff horizontally in half and layer 3 banana slices in the bottom of each. Place a large scoop of ice cream into each puff and top each with 1 teaspoon strawberry preserves. Place the pastry tops over the preserves and spoon 1 tablespoon hot fudge sauce over the top of each. Serve, or cover loosely and keep frozen until ready to use.

Orange Baked Alaska

6 servings

After a big meal, when we need something sweet but not too fill-ing, these stuffed oranges are just the answer! They certainly sound fancy and complicated, but they're 1–2–3 easy.

3 large oranges
1 quart orange sherbet

3 egg whites
1 tablespoon sugar

Cut the oranges crosswise in half. Carefully remove the pulp from the oranges and reserve for another use, taking care to keep the peels intact. Cut a small slice off the bottom of each orange half, without slicing through, so that it sits flat on a rimmed baking sheet. Place a large scoop of sherbet in each orange shell. Place in the freezer until firm. Preheat the oven to 400°F. In a medium-sized bowl, with an electric beater on high speed, beat the egg whites and sugar until stiff peaks form. Remove the sherbet-filled oranges from the freezer and completely cover the sherbet with the egg white mixture (see Note). Bake for 3 to 4 minutes, or until the meringue is lightly browned. Serve immediately, or cover loosely and keep frozen.

NOTE: Make sure the sherbet is frozen solid before covering with the egg white mixture and baking.

Pecan Ice Cream Crepes

10 crepes

Light and fluffy, these crepes deserve high honors for taste and originality—the best part is how simple they are to prepare!

1 cup all-purpose flour
1 tablespoon sugar
¼ teaspoon salt
1 tablespoon butter, melted
2 eggs
1½ cups milk

Vegetable oil for coating skillet
1 block (½ gallon) butter pecan
   ice cream
2 jars (5 ounces each) pecans in
   syrup (wet nuts) (see Note)

In a medium-sized bowl, combine the flour, sugar, salt, melted butter, and eggs; mix with an electric beater on medium speed for 1 to 2 minutes, then add the milk and beat until smooth. Brush a large nonstick skillet with oil and heat over medium-low heat. Pour ¼ cup of batter into the skillet, tilting the skillet to coat the bottom of the pan evenly with the batter; cook for 1 minute or until the edges are brown and the top of the crepe has bubbled up; turn and cook on the second side for 1 minute. Remove the crepe to a platter. Repeat with the remaining batter, coating the skillet with additional vegetable oil as needed. Once the crepes have cooled, remove the block of ice cream from the package and cut crosswise into 5 slices. Cut each slice in half lengthwise, making a total of 10 "logs" of ice cream. Place an ice cream log on the center of each crepe and roll up. Place the filled crepes seam side down on a rimmed baking sheet, then top with the pecans in syrup. Cover and freeze for at least 3 hours before serving.

NOTE: To make your own wet nuts, check out the recipe on page 175. And remember, these crepes can be filled with your favorite flavor of ice cream and topped with almost any kind of sauce.

Chocolate Malted Pops

8 pops

No straws and no blender are needed for this malted. It takes just a few quick strokes, then we pop them in the freezer for solid refreshment.

1 quart vanilla ice cream, softened
¼ cup chocolate malted milk powder
  (see Note)

Eight 5-ounce paper cups
8 nontoxic wooden craft sticks

In a large bowl, combine the ice cream and malted milk powder; stir until well combined. Divide the mixture evenly among the paper cups, then place a wooden stick in the center of each cup. Place in the freezer for at least 3 hours, or until firm. Serve, or wrap each in plastic wrap and keep frozen until ready to serve.

NOTE: Malted milk powder can usually be found next to the cocoa and other drink mixes in the supermarket.

Dreamsicles

6 to 8 pops

These were always a popular alternative to plain ice cream, and this is an easy version that we just blend together and pop in the freezer for a great blast from the past. Sweet dreams. . . .

3 cups orange juice
1 can (5 ounces) evaporated milk
½ cup sugar

1 tablespoon vanilla extract
5 drops red food color (optional)

Blend all the ingredients in a blender or in a large bowl with an electric beater until the sugar has completely dissolved. Pour into ice pop molds and freeze until solid.

NOTE: Don't lose your cool if you don't have ice pop molds; it's the stick part that the kids love, anyway. You can use just about any freezer-safe container to make homemade frozen treats. Try using small paper cups and nontoxic wooden craft sticks—or even plastic spoons—for handles. The cups are perfect for catching drips or for "keeping the rest for later" when their sweet tooth is larger than their appetite.

CMC Ice Cream Sandwiches

about 22 sandwiches

No, it's not a year in Roman numerals—CMC stands for <u>C</u>hocolate <u>M</u>arshmallow <u>C</u>hocolate. And, as a matter of fact, whatever year (or day!) it is, chocolate will always be a favorite.

1½ cups cold milk
1 package (4-serving size) instant
   chocolate pudding and pie filling
1 container (8 ounces) frozen
   whipped topping, thawed

1 cup miniature marshmallows
1 package (9 ounces) chocolate
   wafer cookies

In a large bowl, whisk together the milk and pudding mix until well combined. Stir in the whipped topping and marshmallows. Lay out half the wafers upside down on a cookie sheet and spread the pudding mixture evenly on the wafers, placing about 2 table-spoons on each one. Top with the remaining wafers, forming sandwiches, and lightly press the wafers together. Freeze for 6 hours, then wrap each one individually and return to the freezer until ready to serve.

NOTE: These will keep for up to 2 weeks in the freezer. Why not get creative? If you've got some chopped nuts, semisweet chocolate chips, or peanut butter chips on hand, why not add them to the filling?

Ice Cream Tacos

8 tacos

Not everything from South of the Border is "hot." Sometimes the "hottest" things are as cool as ice—ice cream, that is.

8 frozen round waffles, thawed	½ cup hot fudge sauce
1 quart chocolate ice cream, softened	8 maraschino cherries
½ cup miniature marshmallows	

Warm the waffles according to the package directions. While still warm, gently fold each in half, like a taco. Place in a 7" × 11" baking dish, squeezing into rows so that they retain their shape (see illustration). In a large bowl, combine the ice cream and marshmallows until well mixed, then evenly scoop into the "taco shells." Spoon the fudge sauce over the ice cream and top each with a cherry. Cover and freeze until firm. Serve, or keep frozen until ready to serve.

NOTE: Go wild! Top these with any of your other favorites, like flaked coconut that has been colored with green food color to look like lettuce. (Get the picture?!)

Stuffed Donuts

6 donuts

We all have our special requests when it comes to donuts. Some prefer glazed, some frosted, others . . . fruit-filled. And now it's time to add ice cream–filled donuts to the list!

6 plain cake donuts (see Note)   ½ cup rainbow sprinkles
1 quart chocolate ice cream

Cut the donuts horizontally in half and place a large scoop of ice cream on half of each donut. Replace the other half of each donut and lightly press the donut halves together. Place the sprinkles in a shallow dish and roll the donut edges in the sprinkles, coating the ice cream. Place on a cookie sheet and freeze for 2 hours, or until firm. Serve, or wrap each in plastic wrap and keep frozen until ready to serve.

NOTE: The options are limitless with these ice cream treats. You can use any type of cake donut—powdered, sugared, or cinnamon—and any flavor of ice cream. And go ahead and use any kinds of sprinkles, miniature chocolate chips, or even chopped nuts to coat the ice cream.

Chocolate-Cherry-Surprise Cupcakes

18 cupcakes

Have the kids help make these on a rainy afternoon and watch the sun come out with their every bite!

1 package (18.25 ounces) chocolate cake mix, batter prepared according to the package directions (see Note)
1 jar (10 ounces) maraschino cherries, drained

1 quart vanilla ice cream, softened
½ cup (3 ounces) miniature semisweet chocolate chips
1 container (16 ounces) milk chocolate frosting

Bake the cake batter according to the package directions for 18 cupcakes; let cool completely. Carefully slice off the top of each cooled cupcake and set aside. Hollow out the center of the cupcakes, reserving the cake for another use. Slice 9 of the maraschino cherries in half and set aside. Coarsely chop the remaining cherries and combine with the ice cream and chocolate chips in a medium-sized bowl until well mixed. Fill the hollowed-out cupcakes with the ice cream mixture, then replace the tops. Freeze for 1 hour, or until firm. Frost each cupcake and top with a reserved maraschino cherry half. Serve, or cover and keep frozen until ready to serve.

NOTE: You know, if you'd rather not bake the cupcakes yourself, you can start with store-bought cupcakes. They'll be great, too. Oh, and usually by the time I finish these cupcakes, the hollowed-out centers of the cupcakes have already been eaten. But if they haven't, you can crumble the cake and add it to vanilla pudding to create Dalmatian-spotted pudding.

Scoopable Delights

Lemon Blizzard

about 1½ quarts

When we just want something cool to hit the spot—without filling us up—this is the perfect choice!

4 cups water
2 cups sugar
1 tablespoon grated lemon peel

1 cup fresh lemon juice (from about 6 lemons) (see Note)

In a large saucepan, bring the water, sugar, and lemon peel to a boil over high heat. Add the lemon juice and reduce the heat to medium; cook for 5 minutes. Pour into a 2-quart baking dish and cool to room temperature. Cover and freeze for 2 to 3 hours, until the mixture has frozen 1 inch in from the sides of the pan. Remove from the freezer and mix well, being sure to blend the ice crystals with the remaining mixture. Place in an airtight storage container, seal, and freeze for 6 to 8 hours, or until firm.

NOTE: The flavor is definitely best with fresh lemon juice, but bottled lemon juice can also be used.

Banana Slush

about 1 pint

It's easy to see why everyone will go "bananas" over this!

3 ripe bananas   2 tablespoons lemon juice
3 tablespoons honey

In a food processor that has been fitted with its metal cutting blade, combine all the ingredients and process for 15 seconds, or until smooth. Pour the mixture into an airtight storage container, seal, and freeze for at least 3 hours, or until firm.

NOTE: This is the perfect dessert to make when you have extra ripe bananas on hand.

Zesty Orange Sorbet

about 1 quart

Squeeze this one into your snack plans and you know everyone will be eating with zest!

½ cup sugar
1 envelope (0.25 ounce) unflavored
   gelatin

3 cups orange juice, divided
   (see Note)
1 teaspoon grated orange peel

In a medium-sized bowl, combine the sugar and gelatin; set aside. In a small saucepan, bring 1 cup orange juice to a boil over high heat, then add the gelatin mixture and stir until dissolved. Add the remaining orange juice and the grated orange peel; mix well. Pour into a shallow pan, cover, and freeze for 2 to 3 hours, until firm. Break into medium-sized pieces and place in the bowl of a food processor that has been fitted with its metal cutting blade. Process until the mixture is smooth, then spoon into an airtight storage container. Seal and freeze for 3 to 4 hours, or until firm.

NOTE: Should you use fresh-squeezed orange juice or juice from a carton? Either tastes good here.

Simple Peach Sorbet

about 1 quart

Here's a two-step that's too easy for words!

1 can (29 ounces) peaches in heavy syrup

1 tablespoon orange juice

Place the unopened can of peaches in the freezer until frozen solid, about 24 hours. Submerge the unopened can in very hot tap water for 1 minute. Open the can and pour any thawed syrup into the bowl of a food processor that has been fitted with its metal cutting blade. Remove the frozen fruit from the can and cut into large chunks; place in the food processor and add the orange juice. Process until smooth, scraping down the sides as needed. Serve immediately, or spoon into an airtight storage container; seal and keep frozen until ready to serve.

NOTE: For an even more heavenly flavor, substitute 1 tablespoon peach schnapps for the orange juice. This is so easy, you might even want to try making other sorbet flavors, using canned pears or apricots.

Sinful Chocolate Sherbet

about 1 quart

Sinfully rich, yet feathery light.

¾ cup sugar
½ cup unsweetened cocoa
½ cup hot water

2 cups milk
¼ cup cold water

In a small saucepan, combine the sugar and cocoa. Place over low heat and slowly stir in the hot water. Continue stirring for 2 to 3 minutes, or until the sugar is dissolved and the cocoa is thoroughly blended. Remove from the heat and gradually stir in the milk. Pour into a 9" × 13" baking dish, cover, and freeze for 3 to 4 hours, or until firm. Break up the frozen mixture and place in the bowl of a food processor that has been fitted with its metal cutting blade, or a blender. Add the cold water and process for 2 to 3 minutes, until smooth and light-colored. Pour into an airtight storage container. Seal and freeze for at least 2 hours, or until firm.

NOTE: For a lower-fat sherbet, use low-fat milk instead of whole milk.

Frozen Custard

about 1 quart

For a perfect dessert or a satisfying snack, this blast from the past will be a hands-down winner scoop after scoop!

4 cups (1 quart) milk	3 eggs
1 cup sugar	1 tablespoon vanilla extract

In a large saucepan, combine the milk, sugar, and eggs. Cook over medium heat for 12 to 15 minutes, until the mixture comes to a boil, whisking frequently. Once the mixture boils, whisk constantly for 5 to 6 more minutes, until slightly thickened. Whisk in the vanilla and remove from the heat; allow to cool. Place in a shallow dish, cover, and freeze for at least 2 hours, until firm. Break into medium-sized chunks and place in the bowl of a food processor that has been fitted with its metal cutting blade. Process until the mixture is smooth, then spoon into an airtight storage container. Seal and freeze for 3 to 4 more hours, or until firm.

NOTE: For chocolate chip frozen custard, stir in 1 cup (6 ounces) miniature semisweet chocolate chips after processing.

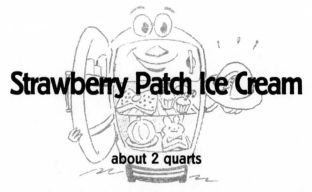

Strawberry Patch Ice Cream

about 2 quarts

Tastes so fresh, they'll think you got these berries straight from the patch—only you'll know they came from the freezer case.

1 can (14 ounces) sweetened
   condensed milk
1 tablespoon vanilla extract
2 drops red food color (optional)

1 package (20 ounces) frozen
   strawberries, thawed and mashed
2 cups (1 pint) heavy cream

In a large bowl, combine the sweetened condensed milk, vanilla, and the food color, if desired. Stir in the strawberries and mix until thoroughly combined. In a medium-sized bowl, with an electric beater on medium speed, beat the cream until stiff peaks form. Gently fold the cream into the strawberry mixture until thoroughly combined. Place in an airtight storage container and freeze for 8 hours, or until firm.

NOTE: Add more or less of the food color, depending on the natural color of the frozen strawberries and the color of ice cream desired.

Butter-Rum Ice Cream

about 2 quarts

My mom always kept butter-rum hard candies in her purse for my sister and me, so I grew up loving that rich flavor. Now I like to use them to give store-bought ice cream a homemade touch. And this one's got a real kick, too!

½ cup dark rum
½ cup (1 stick) unsalted butter
1 package (6.25 ounces) butter-rum
   hard candy, finely crushed

½ gallon vanilla ice cream, softened

In a medium-sized saucepan, combine the rum, butter, and crushed candy. Bring to a slow boil over medium heat and cook for 6 to 8 minutes, until the candy melts and the mixture looks like caramel sauce, stirring constantly. Remove from the heat and allow to cool to room temperature, about 30 minutes. When cooled, stir the sauce again until well mixed. Place the ice cream in a large bowl and swirl in the sauce until completely marbleized. Place in an airtight storage container. Seal and freeze until ready to serve.

NOTE: Go ahead and make this rum-raisin ice cream simply by adding 1 cup raisins to the saucepan after the candy has melted.

Ice Cream Mix-ins

mix-ins for 1 quart ice cream

Every kid dreams of working in an ice cream shop—with all those yummy goodies to taste. Wouldn't it be fun to turn your kitchen into your very own ice cream shop? It's easy—all you need is ice cream and a little imagination for a fantasy come true!

TUTTI-FRUTTI GUM ICE CREAM

1 quart vanilla ice cream, softened

4 packages (0.5 ounce each) tiny rainbow-colored candy-coated gum

RASPBERRY CHIP ICE CREAM

1 quart vanilla ice cream, softened
¼ cup seedless red raspberry preserves

½ cup (3 ounces) miniature semisweet chocolate chips

STRAWBERRY COCONUT CHIP ICE CREAM

1 quart strawberry ice cream, softened
1 cup flaked coconut

¼ cup (1½ ounces) miniature semisweet chocolate chips

HALLOWEEN-LEFTOVER ICE CREAM

1 quart vanilla ice cream, softened

2 cups chopped leftover Halloween candy

continued

ROOT BEER FLOAT ICE CREAM

1 quart vanilla ice cream, softened
1 container (8 ounces) frozen
   whipped topping, thawed

1 cup finely crushed root beer–
   flavored candy

LEMON RIPPLE ICE CREAM

1 quart vanilla ice cream, softened

1 jar (10 ounces) lemon curd
   (see Note)

For each ice cream mix-in, place the softened ice cream in a large bowl and add the remaining ingredient(s). Stir, letting the ingredients swirl together rather than being totally blended. Place in an airtight storage container. Seal and freeze for at least 3 hours, or until firm.

NOTE: What a great rainy-day activity to do with the kids! Experiment with your favorite mix-ins—the possibilities are endless! Oh—lemon curd is usually found with the jams and jellies in the supermarket.

Cool Creations

Chocolate Napoleons

9 to 12 servings

Ready for flaky layers of pastry overstuffed with a decadent chocolate filling? Good, because here it is . . . but it goes down so easily that you just might need to make more than one per person!

2 sheets puff pastry
  (one 17¼-ounce box)
2 packages (4 servings each) instant
  chocolate pudding and pie filling
1¾ cups cold milk, divided

1 container (8 ounces) frozen
  whipped topping, thawed
2 cups confectioners' sugar
¼ teaspoon unsweetened cocoa

Preheat the oven to 400°F. Bake the pastry sheets according to the package directions; let cool. In a medium-sized bowl, combine the chocolate pudding mix and 1½ cups milk; whisk until thickened, then fold in the whipped topping. Spread over 1 layer of the pastry. Place the other pastry flat side up on top of the pudding. Place a cookie sheet on top and press down to distribute the pudding evenly and flatten the pastry, just until the filling begins to ooze out the sides. In a medium-sized bowl, whisk the confectioners' sugar and the remaining ¼ cup milk until a smooth icing is formed. Reserve 2 tablespoons of the icing and set aside. Pour the remaining icing over the top of the pastry and spread to the edges. Stir the cocoa powder into the reserved icing until well blended. Drizzle over the white icing. Freeze for 4 hours, or until firm. Cut into squares and serve, or cover loosely and keep chilled until ready to serve.

Bakery-Style Éclairs

10 éclairs

Looking for something sensational to round out your special dinner? It'll make your company feel really special when they find out you made these yourself.

1 cup water
½ cup (1 stick) butter, cut into quarters
¼ teaspoon salt
1 cup all-purpose flour
4 eggs, at room temperature

2 cups (1 pint) heavy cream
1 package (4-serving size) instant vanilla pudding and pie filling
1 cup confectioners' sugar
3 tablespoons unsweetened cocoa
2 tablespoons plus 1 teaspoon milk

Preheat the oven to 400°F. In a medium-sized saucepan, bring the water, butter, and salt to a boil over medium-high heat. Add the flour all at once and stir quickly with a wooden spoon until the mixture forms a ball. Remove from the heat. Add 1 egg to the mixture and beat hard with the wooden spoon to blend. Add the remaining eggs one at a time, beating well after each addition; each egg must be completely blended before the next egg is added. As you beat the dough, it will change from looking almost curdled to smooth. When it is smooth, spoon the dough into a large resealable plastic storage bag and, using scissors, snip off one corner of the bag, making a 1-inch-wide cut. Gently squeeze the bag to form ten 1" × 4" dough logs about 2 inches apart on an ungreased large rimmed baking sheet. Bake for 40 to 45 minutes, until golden and puffy. Remove to a wire rack to cool. In a large bowl, with an electric beater on medium speed, beat the cream until stiff peaks form. Fold in the pudding mix and set aside. In a small bowl, stir together the confectioners' sugar, cocoa, and milk into a smooth icing. Cut the éclair shells horizontally in half and spoon the pudding mixture evenly into the bottom of each. Replace the tops of the éclair shells and spread the cocoa mixture over the tops. Cover loosely and chill for at least 1 hour before serving.

Tiramisù

9 servings

Italian restaurants everywhere feature this luscious dessert on their menus. And now we can make it at home with no fuss. What a great treat for spaghetti night!

1 cup warm water
4 teaspoons instant coffee granules
¼ cup coffee-flavored liqueur
   (see Note)
1 package (8 ounces) cream cheese,
   softened
¼ cup sour cream
2 tablespoons heavy cream

⅓ cup sugar
½ cup refrigerated egg substitute
   (the equivalent of 2 eggs)
2 cups frozen whipped topping,
   thawed
2 packages (3 ounces each)
   ladyfingers
1 teaspoon unsweetened cocoa

In a small bowl, combine the water, coffee granules, and liqueur; stir to dissolve the coffee, and set aside. In a large bowl, blend the cream cheese, sour cream, and heavy cream until smooth. Add the sugar and egg substitute; mix well, then fold in the whipped topping. Split 1 package of ladyfingers and quickly dip each into the coffee mixture one at a time; line the bottom of an 8-inch square glass baking dish with the moistened ladyfingers. Spoon half of the cream mixture evenly over them. Split the second package of ladyfingers and, working quickly, dip each in the coffee mixture one at a time; place them over the cream layer and top with the remaining cream mixture. Sprinkle with the cocoa powder. Cover and chill for 3 to 4 hours, or overnight.

NOTE: If you prefer to omit the coffee-flavored liqueur, just use 1¼ cups strong black coffee instead of the water, instant coffee, and liqueur. Got any leftover coffee? This sure is a great way to give it new life!

158

Sweet Potato Surprise

12 to 15 servings

If you keep it between us, I'll tell you the surprise—it's how easy it is to make this surprisingly yummy treat!

1¼ cups self-rising flour
⅔ cup chopped pecans, divided
1 cup (2 sticks) unsalted butter, melted, divided
1 container (16 ounces) frozen whipped topping, thawed

1 package (8 ounces) cream cheese, softened
¾ cup sugar
2 cans (29 ounces each) sweet potatoes, drained and mashed
1½ teaspoons vanilla extract

Preheat the oven to 350°F. In a medium-sized bowl, combine the flour, ⅓ cup pecans, and ½ cup melted butter; mix well. Spread into the bottom of a 9" × 13" baking dish. Bake for 15 to 18 minutes, until lightly browned. Cool to room temperature. Set aside 1½ cups of the whipped topping. In a medium-sized bowl, combine the remaining whipped topping, the cream cheese, and sugar; mix well. In another medium-sized bowl, combine the sweet potatoes, the remaining ½ cup melted butter, and the vanilla; mix well. Spread the cream cheese mixture over the cooled crust, then spread the sweet potato mixture over the top. Spread the reserved whipped topping over the potatoes and sprinkle with the remaining ⅓ cup pecans. Cover and chill for at least 2 hours before serving.

NOTE: If you prefer, you can substitute walnuts for the pecans.

Crème Caramel

8 to 10 servings

Did you ever wonder how the fancy restaurants make those elegant-looking desserts? This is one we see all the time, but would never dream of attempting at home. Well, why not? With just four ingredients and a few basic steps, you're home free!

¾ cup sugar, divided
4 eggs

1 teaspoon vanilla extract
2 cups milk

Preheat the oven to 350°F. In a small nonstick skillet, stir ½ cup sugar over medium heat for about 6 minutes, until completely melted and caramel-colored, stirring occasionally. Immediately pour the melted sugar into a 9-inch glass pie plate, coating the bottom of the plate. **(Be careful when working with the melted sugar; it is very hot.)** In a medium-sized bowl, beat the eggs with the vanilla. In a small bowl, combine the milk with the remaining ¼ cup sugar, then beat into the egg mixture. Pour over the caramelized sugar. Place the pie plate in a large shallow pan. Pour hot water into the pan to come about halfway up the side of the pie plate. Bake for 40 minutes, or until a knife inserted in the center comes out clean. Remove from the water and let cool for 20 minutes, then cover and chill for at least 4 hours, or overnight. To serve, invert the custard onto a 10- to 12-inch rimmed serving plate. Cut into wedges and drizzle with the caramel.

NOTE: Be careful when inverting the pie plate. The best way is to place the serving plate upside down over the pie plate and, holding the two together tightly, turn them over quickly. Then slowly remove the pie plate.

160

Edible Pumpkin Mousse Baskets

6 baskets

Company's coming, and you want to bake something unforget-table—an edible basket of goodness is the answer.

Six 8-inch flour tortillas
Nonstick baking spray
½ cup plus 2 tablespoons sugar
1 can (16 ounces) solid-pack pure
   pumpkin
1 package (6-serving size) instant
   vanilla pudding and pie filling

¼ cup milk
1 teaspoon ground cinnamon
2 cups frozen whipped topping,
   thawed

Preheat the oven to 425°F. Spray the tortillas on both sides with the baking spray. Sprinkle ½ teaspoon sugar on each side and place each in a large muffin cup, forming 6 baskets. Bake for 8 to 10 minutes, or until light golden; allow to cool. In a medium-sized bowl, with an electric beater on medium speed, beat the pumpkin, pudding mix, milk, and cinnamon until well blended. Fold in the whipped topping until thoroughly blended, then spoon into the tortilla baskets. Cover loosely and chill until ready to serve.

NOTE: Top with some additional whipped topping or chopped walnuts, if desired.

Special Occasion Chocolate Cups

6 cups

I love these because you can fill and top them with something different every time you make them. I made these for a luncheon recently and served them filled with Sinful Chocolate Sherbet (page 147) and topped with fresh raspberries. You should have seen my guests' excited faces when I brought these out . . . and their satisfied faces after they gobbled them up!

1 cup (6 ounces) semisweet chocolate chips	1 tablespoon vegetable shortening

Place 6 paper baking cups in regular muffin cups. In a small saucepan, heat the chocolate and shortening over low heat for 1 to 2 minutes, stirring, just until the chocolate melts and the mixture is smooth. Allow to cool slightly; the mixture should still be pourable (see Note). Starting at the top edge of each paper cup, spoon the chocolate over the insides of the cups, completely covering the inside of each cup with about 4 teaspoons of the mixture. Chill the cups for 25 to 30 minutes, until firm. Carefully remove the paper from the chocolate and place the cups on a serving plate; chill until ready to use. Before serving, fill with your favorite pudding, mousse, or ice cream.

NOTE: Make sure the chocolate is runny but not so runny that it doesn't stick to the sides of the paper cups.

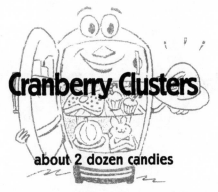

Cranberry Clusters

about 2 dozen candies

What to do with all those fresh cranberries left over from the holidays? No need to wait for company—treat yourself by turning them into candy!

2 tablespoons vegetable shortening
2 packages (6 ounces each) white
    baking bars, cut into chunks
    (see Note)

1 package (12 ounces) fresh
    cranberries, rinsed and dried

In a medium-sized saucepan, melt the shortening over low heat. Add the baking bars and stir continuously until melted. Stir in the cranberries and remove from the heat. Drop by heaping teaspoonfuls onto a waxed paper–lined cookie sheet. Chill for 2 hours, or until hardened. Place in an airtight storage container and keep refrigerated until ready to serve.

NOTE: Two cups (12 ounces) chocolate chips (milk or semisweet) can be used instead of the white baking bars. Or you can use some of each to have a variety of cranberry clusters.

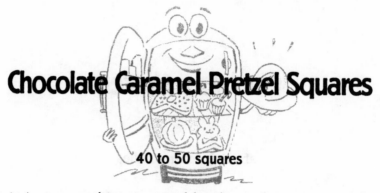

Chocolate Caramel Pretzel Squares

40 to 50 squares

There's just something irresistible about these. It must be the unusual taste combination of chocolate, caramel, and pretzels.

1 cup crushed pretzels
¼ cup plus ⅓ cup butter, melted
1 can (14 ounces) sweetened
    condensed milk

¼ cup sugar
1 cup (6 ounces) semisweet
    chocolate chips, melted

Preheat the oven to 400°F. Line a 7" × 11" baking pan with aluminum foil, letting the ends extend beyond the edges on two opposite sides. Coat the foil with nonstick baking spray. In a small bowl, combine the pretzels and ¼ cup melted butter; mix well and press into the bottom of the pan. Bake for 10 minutes; set aside. In a small saucepan, combine the sweetened condensed milk, sugar, and the remaining ⅓ cup butter; bring to a boil over medium-high heat, stirring constantly. Reduce the heat to medium-low and cook for 10 minutes, or until golden, stirring constantly. Pour the sweetened condensed milk mixture over the crust and chill for 30 minutes, or until firm. Smooth the chocolate over the top and chill for at least 2 hours, until firm. Lift the foil from the pan, then remove the foil and place on a flat cutting surface. Cut into small squares. Serve, or cover and keep chilled until ready to serve.

NOTE: You can also press miniature pretzels into the chocolate while it's still soft, so that each square will have a pretzel on it.

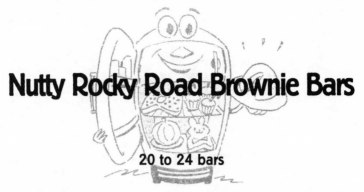

Nutty Rocky Road Brownie Bars

20 to 24 bars

Fudgy? *Yes*! Nutty? *You bet*! Dunkable? *Oh, boy*! One of my favorites? *Yes*! *You bet*! *Oh, boy*!

1 package (22.5 ounces) brownie
   mix, batter prepared according
   to the package directions
1 package (10½ ounces) miniature
   marshmallows

1½ cups (9 ounces) semisweet
   chocolate chips
1 cup crunchy peanut butter
1 tablespoon butter
1½ cups crispy rice cereal

Bake the brownie batter according to the package directions for a 9" × 13" baking dish. Remove from the oven and sprinkle with the marshmallows. Return to the oven and bake for 5 minutes, or until the marshmallows melt; set aside. In a medium-sized saucepan, combine the chocolate chips, peanut butter, and butter and heat over low heat until the chips are melted, stirring constantly. Add the crispy rice cereal; mix well. Spread over the top of the brownies and allow to cool slightly. Cover and chill for at least 2 hours, or until thoroughly chilled. Cut into squares just before serving.

NOTE: For even nuttier brownies, mix ½ cup peanuts in with the cereal.

Almond Toffee Bars

20 to 24 bars

Toffee is such a great flavor! I know everybody'll go nuts over these chewy dessert bars.

1½ cups all-purpose flour
½ cup confectioners' sugar
¾ cup (1½ sticks) cold butter
1 can (14 ounces) sweetened
    condensed milk
1 egg, beaten

1 teaspoon almond extract
6 chocolate-covered toffee candy
    bars (1.4 ounces each), coarsely
    chopped
1 cup chopped almonds

Preheat the oven to 350°F. In a medium-sized bowl, combine the flour and confectioners' sugar. Cut the butter into the mixture until crumbly, then press firmly into the bottom of a 9" × 13" baking pan. Bake for 15 minutes. Meanwhile, in a large bowl, combine the sweetened condensed milk, egg, and almond extract; mix well. Stir in the chopped candy bars and almonds and spread evenly over the hot crust. Bake for 22 to 25 minutes, until golden brown. Let cool; cover and chill until ready to serve. Cut into bars when ready to serve.

NOTE: Wow! Add ½ cup finely chopped almonds to the flour-and-sugar mixture to create an almond-packed crust.

Sunny Lemon Fruit Bites

20 to 24 servings

Weather looking gloomy? Take a bite of these, 'cause their fruity flavor is like a ray of sunshine.

4 cups finely crushed toasted rice cereal	1 can (14 ounces) sweetened condensed milk
½ cup (1 stick) butter, melted	2 cans (15¼ ounces each) fruit cocktail, drained
⅓ cup sugar	1 tablespoon grated lemon rind
1 package (4-serving size) lemon pie filling, prepared according to the package directions (see Note)	1 container (8 ounces) frozen whipped topping, thawed

Preheat the oven to 300°F. In a large bowl, combine the cereal, butter, and sugar. Spread half the mixture into a 9" × 13" baking dish. Bake for 12 to 15 minutes, until light golden; let cool. In a large bowl, combine the pie filling, sweetened condensed milk, fruit cocktail, and lemon rind; stir to blend thoroughly, then spread over the cooled crust. Cover evenly with the whipped topping, then sprinkle with the remaining cereal mixture. Cover and chill for at least 2 hours before serving.

NOTE: Make sure to use lemon pie filling, *not* lemon pudding, for the filling; however, you can use a 16-ounce can of lemon pie filling instead of the packaged mix.

Cranberry Chocolate Chip Bars

20 to 24 bars

You don't have to wait for autumn, 'cause it's always the season for cranberries . . . and boy, can they ever spark up a plain old chocolate chip bar!

1 cup (2 sticks) butter, softened
1 cup firmly packed light brown sugar
2 cups all-purpose flour
1½ cups uncooked old-fashioned oats
2 teaspoons grated orange peel
2 cups (12 ounces) semisweet chocolate chips

1 cup sweetened dried cranberries (see Note)
1 package (8 ounces) cream cheese, softened
1 can (14 ounces) sweetened condensed milk

Preheat the oven to 350°F. In a large bowl, with an electric beater on medium speed, cream the butter and brown sugar until smooth. Beat in the flour, oats, and orange peel; the mixture will be crumbly. With a spoon, stir in the chocolate chips and cranberries. Reserve 2 cups of the mixture and press the remaining mixture into a 9" × 13" baking pan that has been coated with nonstick baking spray. Bake for 15 minutes. Meanwhile, in a medium-sized bowl, with an electric beater on medium speed, beat the cream cheese until smooth, then gradually beat in the sweetened condensed milk. Pour over the hot crust and sprinkle with the reserved oat mixture. Bake for 25 to 30 minutes, until the center of the topping is set. Allow to cool, then cover and chill for at least 2 hours before serving. Cut into bars and serve.

NOTE: Sweetened dried cranberries look like raisins, and they can usually be found near the raisins in the supermarket. If you can't find them, you can use raisins, or leave the fruit out completely.

Sauces and Toppings

Ruby Sauce

about 5 cups

The combination of strawberries and rhubarb makes this sauce a red-letter gem. Its ruby-red color and rich taste make it just right for fancying up any plain dessert.

1 package (20 ounces) frozen
   strawberries, thawed
1 package (20 ounces) frozen
   rhubarb, thawed
1 cup sugar

1 cinnamon stick
¾ cup dry red wine or grape juice
2 teaspoons cornstarch
4 teaspoons water

In a large saucepan, combine the strawberries, rhubarb, sugar, cinnamon stick, and wine. Cover and cook over medium-low heat for 20 minutes. In a small bowl, combine the cornstarch and water, stirring until smooth. Add to the strawberry-rhubarb mixture and stir for 3 to 4 minutes, until thickened. Discard the cinnamon stick and allow the mixture to cool. Cover and chill until ready to serve.

NOTE: Turn ice cream, cake, pudding, or even fresh fruit into a special dessert by topping it with this versatile sauce.

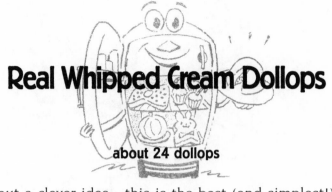

Real Whipped Cream Dollops

about 24 dollops

Talk about a clever idea—this is the best (and simplest!) way to impress company and even treat yourself. So go to it. . . .

1 cup (½ pint) heavy cream   2 teaspoons confectioners' sugar

In a medium-sized bowl, whip the cream and confectioners' sugar with an electric beater on high speed until stiff peaks form. Spoon heaping tablespoon–sized dollops of the whipped cream onto a waxed paper–lined cookie sheet. Freeze for about 1½ hours, until solid. Transfer the dollops to a resealable plastic storage bag, close tightly, and keep in the freezer until ready to use. Just before serving, remove one dollop per treat and allow to thaw before eating.

NOTE: These will last in the freezer for up to 1 month.

Vanilla Sauce

about 4 cups

Drizzle this over your favorite desserts, or be fancy and serve your cakes and other treats sitting in a puddle of it. You can't miss—it's the crowning jewel of any dessert!

3½ cups cold milk
1 package (4-serving size) instant
   vanilla pudding and pie filling

1 teaspoon vanilla extract
3 tablespoons brandy or liqueur, any
   flavor (optional) (see Note)

In a large bowl, combine the milk, pudding mix, and vanilla; whisk until well blended. Add the brandy, if desired, and continue whisking until thoroughly blended. Before using, chill for at least one hour, or until slightly thickened.

NOTE: If you include brandy or liqueur, then keep this as an adults-only sauce.

173

Chocolate Sauce

about 3½ cups

How do we make sure our desserts are the tops? Simple—cover them with everyone's number one favorite topping! (At least it is in *my* house!)

2 cups sugar
¾ cup unsweetened cocoa
¼ cup all-purpose flour
¼ teaspoon salt

2 cups water
1 tablespoon vanilla extract
2 tablespoons butter

In a small bowl, combine the sugar, cocoa, flour, and salt; mix well. In a medium-sized saucepan, combine the water, vanilla, and butter over medium heat. When the butter melts, stir in the sugar mixture and cook until slightly thickened and bubbling. Remove from the heat, let cool, then cover and chill until ready to use.

NOTE: As an ice cream topper, and with cake, too, this chocolate sauce is unbeatable.

Wet Nuts

about 1 cup

If you're from my era, you probably remember how popular these were at the drugstore soda fountain. Now you can bring back an old-fashioned winner when you top your ice cream with these memories.

¼ cup light corn syrup   1 cup pecan halves
2 tablespoons maple syrup

In a small saucepan, combine all the ingredients over low heat and cook for 5 minutes, until well combined, stirring frequently. Allow to cool slightly, then pour into a plastic storage container, cover, and chill for at least 8 hours before using.

NOTE: I take turns—sometimes I make these with walnuts instead of pecans.

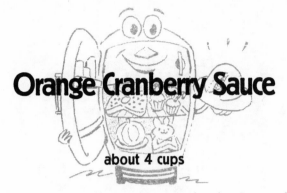

Orange Cranberry Sauce

about 4 cups

I first made this to top slices of pound cake for a Thanksgiving dessert a few years ago. Now I keep some on hand in my fridge for topping all sorts of goodies.

4 cups fresh cranberries
1½ cups orange juice
1 cup sugar

2 tablespoons grated orange peel
2 tablespoons Triple Sec or other
orange-flavored liqueur (optional)

In a medium-sized saucepan, combine the cranberries, orange juice, sugar, and orange peel. Bring to a boil over medium-high heat, then reduce the heat to low and simmer for 10 minutes. Carefully pour into a blender and process until smooth. Pour into a bowl and stir in the liqueur, if desired. Chill for at least 2 hours before serving.

NOTE: This sauce dresses up vanilla ice cream beautifully—both in looks *and* taste!

Sweet 'n' Tart Nectar

about 1½ cups

When you're as "busy as a bee" but want to make something special for dessert, call on this sauce to go with fresh fruit, pound cake, or whatever you whip up.

¼ cup honey
2 tablespoons lemon juice

2 tablespoons orange marmalade
1 cup (½ pint) heavy cream

In a small saucepan, combine the honey, lemon juice, and orange marmalade. Bring to a boil over medium-high heat. Remove to a medium-sized heat-proof bowl and chill until cold. Add the cream and stir until well blended. Serve immediately, or cover and keep chilled until ready to serve.

Delicious Applesauce

about 2 cups

Use Delicious apples and you're gonna be assured of a doubly delicious fresh applesauce.

5 large Red Delicious apples (about
   2 pounds), cored and quartered
½ cup water

⅓ cup sugar
½ teaspoon ground cinnamon

In a medium-sized saucepan, combine all the ingredients. Bring to a boil over medium-high heat, then reduce the heat to low, cover, and simmer for 25 to 30 minutes, or until the apples are tender. Allow to cool slightly, then transfer the apple mixture in batches to a blender and process on low speed for 15 to 20 seconds, until smooth and well blended. Place in an airtight storage container. Seal and chill until ready to serve.

NOTE: As a side dish or a topping, homemade applesauce will be yours in no time!

White Russian Sauce

about 1½ cups

No, this isn't a drink, it's a dessert topping that'll win you raves every time.

One 2-ounce white baking bar   ¼ cup coffee-flavored liqueur
1 cup (½ pint) heavy cream, divided

In a heavy saucepan, combine the baking bar and ½ cup heavy cream and heat over low heat until the bar is melted and the mixture is smooth, stirring constantly. Remove from the heat and allow to cool completely. In a medium-sized bowl, with an electric beater on medium speed, beat the remaining ½ cup cream until stiff peaks form. Add the melted baking bar mixture and the coffee-flavored liqueur and stir until thoroughly combined. Cover and chill until ready to serve.

NOTE: Served with chocolate cake or as a topping for coffee ice cream . . . mmm, mmm!

Treats by the Calendar

Champagne Dessert Cocktails

8 servings

You'll be the toast of the town when you ring in the new year with this "adults-only" version of our old friend, gelatin.

2 packages (4 servings each)
   lemon-flavored gelatin
2 cups boiling water

2 cups champagne
8 strawberries, hulled

In a large bowl, dissolve the gelatin in the boiling water; let cool for 10 minutes. Add the champagne and chill for 40 to 45 minutes, until slightly thickened. Reserve 1 cup of the gelatin mixture and spoon the remaining gelatin mixture evenly into 8 champagne flutes or parfait glasses. Place 1 strawberry in each glass. In a small bowl, with an electric beater on high speed, beat the reserved 1 cup gelatin mixture until fluffy and doubled in volume. Spoon evenly into the glasses, then cover and chill for at least 2 hours, until set.

NOTE: This is a perfect way to enjoy leftover champagne. It's also good for those times when you want to serve a sparkling dessert.

183

FEBRUARY

Red Velvet Cake

12 to 16 servings

For Valentine's Day, or any day you're ready to paint the town red, this cake's the answer.

1½ cups vegetable shortening
1½ cups sugar
2 eggs
2½ cups all-purpose flour
1 tablespoon unsweetened cocoa
1 teaspoon baking soda
1 teaspoon salt

1 cup buttermilk
1 tablespoon vanilla extract
1 teaspoon white vinegar
2 tablespoons red food color
    (one 1-ounce bottle) (see Note)
Cream Cheese Pecan Frosting
    (next page)

Preheat the oven to 350°F. In a large bowl, with an electric beater on medium speed, beat the shortening, sugar, and eggs for 2 to 3 minutes, until light and fluffy. Add the flour, cocoa, baking soda, and salt and continue beating until well mixed. Gradually add the buttermilk, vanilla, and vinegar, beating for 2 to 3 minutes, until thoroughly combined. With a spoon, stir in the food color until thoroughly mixed. Spoon the batter evenly into three 8-inch round cake pans that have been coated with nonstick baking spray and lightly floured. Bake for 30 to 35 minutes, until a wooden toothpick inserted in the center comes out clean. Allow to cool slightly, then remove to a wire rack to cool completely. Place 1 cake layer on a serving platter and frost the top. Place another layer over the first and frost the top. Place the remaining layer over that and frost the top and the sides. Cover loosely and chill for at least 2 hours before serving.

NOTE: Yes, it takes 2 *tablespoons* of red food color to give this its rich red hue.

184

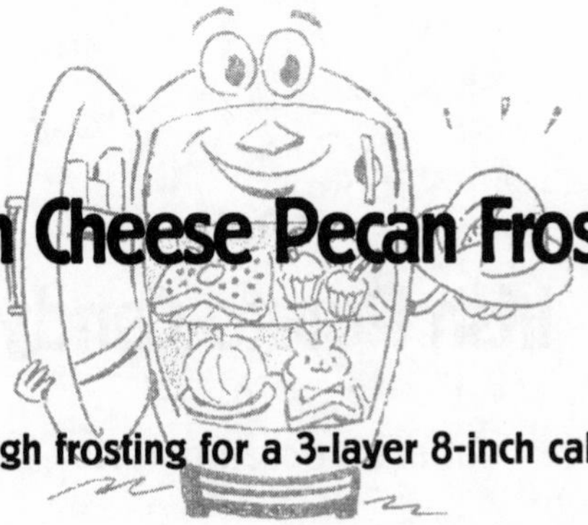

Cream Cheese Pecan Frosting

enough frosting for a 3-layer 8-inch cake

1 package (8 ounces) cream cheese, softened
½ cup (1 stick) butter, softened

2½ cups confectioners' sugar
1 teaspoon vanilla extract
1 cup chopped pecans

In a medium-sized bowl, with an electric beater on medium speed, beat the cream cheese, butter, confectioners' sugar, and vanilla. Increase the speed to high and beat for 1 to 2 more minutes, until the frosting is smooth. Stir in the pecans until thoroughly mixed. Use immediately, or cover and chill until ready to use, allowing the frosting to soften before using.

NOTE: Make sure to use only a thin layer of this when you frost the cake. That way, you'll be able to see the red color of the cake under the frosting.

Irish Potato Candy

about 3 dozen candies

There's something really special about homemade candies—no two are alike, but they all satisfy our craving for sweets!

¼ cup (½ stick) butter, softened
4 ounces cream cheese, softened
   (see Note)
1 teaspoon vanilla extract
1 package (16 ounces) confectioners'
   sugar

1 package (7 ounces) flaked coconut
   (about 2½ cups)
1½ teaspoons ground cinnamon

In a large bowl, with an electric beater on medium speed, cream together the butter and cream cheese. Beat in the vanilla and confectioners' sugar. With a spoon, stir in the coconut. Roll the mixture between your hands to form small potato-shaped candies, or roll into small balls. Place the cinnamon in a shallow dish. Roll the balls in the cinnamon, then place on a cookie sheet, cover, and chill for about 1 hour, until firm.

NOTE: Make sure to use regular cream cheese, not a whipped or reduced-fat type. And if you prefer "dirtier" potatoes, roll the candies a second time in additional cinnamon after they've chilled.

APRIL
Easter Bunny Cake

20 to 24 servings

Hop to it! And, boy, will the gang be glad you did!

1 package (18.25 ounces) white cake mix, batter prepared according to the package directions
2 cups (1 pint) heavy cream
⅓ cup confectioners' sugar
½ teaspoon vanilla extract

1 cup flaked coconut
2 drops red food color
3 maraschino cherries
1 tube (0.68 ounce) black decorating gel

Bake the cake batter according to the package directions for one 8-inch square pan and one 8-inch round pan, making sure the batter is divided equally so the layers are the same height. Let cool slightly, then remove to a wire rack to cool completely. Place the round layer on a large platter. Cut the square layer as shown in illustration 1. Place the cut pieces of cake on the platter as shown in illustration 2, forming ears and a bow tie. In a medium-sized bowl, with an electric beater on medium speed, beat the cream, confectioners' sugar, and vanilla until stiff peaks form. Frost the cake with the whipped cream. In a small bowl, combine the coconut and food

1.

color, stirring until the coconut turns pink. Place inside the ears and around the sides of the cake as shown in illustration 3. Place

2.

Whipped cream

Pink coconut

3.

the cherries on top, forming two eyes and a nose, and use the gel to make the whiskers, mouth, and the center of the bow tie as shown in illustration 3. Cover loosely and chill until ready to serve.

NOTE: Be creative and feel free to change the color of the coconut or other decorations.

Bouquet of Flowers Cake

12 to 16 servings

On Mother's Day, or any time you want to say "I love you" with flowers, this one really takes the cake for originality.

3 tablespoons rainbow sprinkles
1 package (18.25 ounces) yellow cake
   mix, batter prepared according
   to the package directions
2 cups (1 pint) heavy cream
¼ cup confectioners' sugar

1 package (7 ounces) flaked coconut
   (about 2½ cups)
¼ cup granulated sugar
12 large sugar-coated gumdrops
   (3 green and 9 assorted colors)
   (see Note)

Stir the sprinkles into the cake batter and bake according to the package directions for two 8-inch round cake pans. Let cool slightly, then remove from the pans and allow to cool completely on wire racks. In a large bowl, with an electric beater on medium speed, beat the cream and confectioners' sugar until stiff peaks form. Place 1 cake layer on a serving plate and frost the top with whipped cream. Place the second layer on the first and frost the top and sides of the cake with the remaining whipped cream. Sprinkle the coconut over the entire cake. Sprinkle a cutting board with the granulated sugar. With a rolling pin, roll the gumdrops out over the sugar until they form circles about 3 inches in diameter, pressing the flattened gumdrops into the sugar as they get sticky. Set the green gumdrops aside. Pinch each remaining gumdrop in the center, gathering it up to form a "flower." Place the pinched sides down in a bouquet in the center of the cake. Cut the green gumdrops into leaf shapes and place around the flowers. Cover loosely and chill for at least 2 hours before serving.

NOTE: Make sure to use large gumdrops or use more small ones to create a bouquet of miniature flowers.

JUNE
Bow Tie Cake

10 to 12 servings

A special cake for Father's Day, or any time you want to be "dressed for the occasion."

1 package (22.5 ounces) brownie mix, batter prepared according to the package directions
1 quart chocolate ice cream, softened
1 container (12 ounces) frozen whipped topping, thawed

1 teaspoon yellow food color
One 3-inch round sugar cookie
¼ cup candy-coated chocolate candies

Preheat the oven to 350°F. Pour the brownie batter into an 8-inch square baking pan that has been lined with aluminum foil and coated with nonstick baking spray. Bake for 40 to 45 minutes, or until a wooden toothpick inserted in the center comes out clean. Allow to cool completely, then spread the ice cream evenly over the top, covering the brownies completely. Cover and freeze for at least 4 hours, until firm. Invert the pan onto a cutting board and remove the pan and foil. Slice the brownie diagonally in half (see illustration 1). Place the 2 triangles together on a serving plate to form a bow tie, as shown in illustration 2. In a medium-sized bowl, combine the whipped topping and food color, stirring until uniform in color. Frost the bow tie with the whipped topping. Place the cookie in the center of the tie and decorate the bow tie with the chocolate candies as shown in illustration 3 (see Note). Cover loosely and freeze for at least 2 hours before serving.

continued

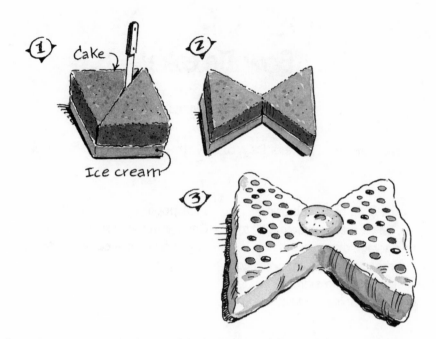

NOTE: This "tie," like any of Dad's, can be decorated with stripes, polka dots, or even a paisley pattern. Let your creativity shine.

Patriotic Parfaits

4 servings

Cool the fireworks with a burst of fresh fruit flavor.

1 cup (½ pint) heavy cream
1 tablespoon Triple Sec or other
   orange-flavored liqueur or
   orange juice

¼ cup confectioners' sugar
1 pint fresh blueberries
½ pint fresh raspberries

In a medium-sized bowl, whisk together the cream, liqueur, and confectioners' sugar until slightly thickened. Divide the blueberries equally among 4 parfait glasses. Drizzle three quarters of the cream mixture over the blueberries, then top with the raspberries. Drizzle with the remaining cream mixture, then cover and chill until ready to serve.

NOTE: Instead of making this in parfait glasses, you can also serve it over slices of angel food cake to create a heavenly dessert.

AUGUST
Frozen "Watermelon"

10 to 12 servings

In the dog days of summer, there's nothing more refreshing than cool watermelon. This one's so cool, it's frozen.

3 pints vanilla ice cream, slightly
   softened
3 pints raspberry sherbet, softened
½ cup (3 ounces) miniature
   semisweet chocolate chips

14 drops green food color
2 cups frozen whipped topping,
   thawed

Line an 8-cup mold or mixing bowl completely with aluminum foil. Working quickly, spread the vanilla ice cream 1 inch thick over the bottom and sides of the bowl. (It'll probably slide down the sides a bit.) Immediately place in the freezer and freeze for about 1 hour. When the ice cream has become somewhat hard, but not frozen solid, spread it all the way up the sides to the top of the bowl;

then replace it in the freezer for about 1 hour, until firm. Place the raspberry sherbet in a medium-sized bowl and add the chocolate chips; blend until evenly mixed. Place in the vanilla ice cream–lined bowl. Cover with plastic wrap and freeze overnight, or until completely hard. When ready to serve, in a small bowl, mix the green food color with the whipped topping until evenly blended. Remove the mold from the freezer and invert onto a platter larger than the mold. Remove the mold and peel off the foil. Spread the whipped topping evenly over the ice cream and serve immediately, or freeze until the topping is firm, then cover and keep frozen until ready to serve. Cut into wedges, just like fresh watermelon.

Dirt Cups

10 servings

It's back-to-school time, so why not have a little fun with the kids when they get home? They'll really "dig" making these.

1 package (4-serving size) instant chocolate pudding and pie filling, prepared according to the package directions
1 container (8 ounces) frozen whipped topping, thawed

1 package (16 ounces) cream-filled chocolate sandwich cookies, finely crushed
Gummy worms and frogs, candy flowers, chopped peanuts, and/or granola for decoration (optional)

Allow the pudding to thicken for 5 minutes, then stir in the whipped topping and half of the crushed cookies. Place 1 tablespoon of the remaining crushed cookies in each of ten 9-ounce paper cups. Fill each cup three-quarters full with the pudding mixture, then top with the remaining crushed cookies. Cover and chill for about 1 hour before serving. Decorate as desired.

NOTE: You can crush the cookies by hand or in a food processor. To make Sand Cups, substitute vanilla pudding for the chocolate pudding and a 12-ounce package of cream-filled vanilla sandwich cookies or vanilla wafers, finely crushed, for the chocolate sandwich cookies. Use gummy worms and sharks and/or chopped peanuts for decoration.

Halloween Pumpkin Cake

20 to 24 servings

For that Halloween party or simply as an autumn treat for the kids, there's no trick to this pumpkin-shaped cake.

2 packages (18.25 ounces each) devil's food cake mix, batter prepared according to the package directions
1 package (4-serving size) instant vanilla pudding and pie filling
1½ cups cold milk

¾ teaspoon red food color, divided
¾ teaspoon yellow food color, divided
2 containers (16 ounces each) white frosting
4 drops green food color

Bake the cake batter in two Bundt pans according to the package directions. Let cool slightly, then remove from the pans and allow to cool completely on a wire rack. While the cakes are cooling, in a medium-sized bowl, whisk together the pudding mix and milk. Add ¼ teaspoon red food color and ¼ teaspoon yellow food color to the pudding and whisk until it turns orange; cover and chill. After the cakes have cooled, place 1 cake on a serving platter, flat side up. Without cutting through the bottom of the cake, make a vertical cut ½ inch from the outside edge of the cake all the way around the cake, then make another vertical cut (parallel to the first one) ½ inch from the inside edge of the cake all around the cake, as shown in illustration 1. Gently remove the cake between the 2 cuts to form a trench, being careful not to tear the bottom of the cake; set aside. Fill the trench with the pudding. Place the other cake, flat side down, on top of the first cake, lining up the edges. Set aside ½ cup of the frosting. In a medium-sized bowl, combine the remaining frosting with the remaining ½ teaspoon red and ½ teaspoon yellow food color; mix well. In a small bowl, combine the reserved ½ cup frosting with the green food color, stirring until well blended. Fill the center hole of the cake with the reserved cake pieces as shown in illustration 2, allowing one long piece to stick out the top, forming a stem. Frost the cake lightly with the orange frosting; the ridges in the cake should still be visible. Frost the stem with the green frosting. Chill for at least 4 hours before serving.

NOTE: Use some decorating gel to turn this pumpkin into your favorite jack-o'-lantern.

1. Out with the cake

In with the Pudding

2. In with the cake pieces!

3. Frost to look like me!

NOVEMBER
Pumpkin Nut Torte

12 to 16 servings

At Thanksgiving, everyone looks forward to having a slice of good old pumpkin pie . . . but here's another delicious way to enjoy our favorite holiday dessert flavors.

1 cup chopped walnuts
1 package (18.25 ounces) spice cake mix, batter prepared according to the package directions
1 can (16 ounces) solid-pack pure pumpkin

¾ cup confectioners' sugar
2 teaspoons ground cinnamon
½ teaspoon ground cloves
¼ teaspoon ground nutmeg
1 container (16 ounces) frozen whipped topping, thawed

Add the chopped walnuts to the batter and bake according to the package directions for two 9-inch round cake pans. Allow to cool completely on wire racks. In a large bowl, combine the pumpkin, confectioners' sugar, cinnamon, cloves, and nutmeg until thoroughly mixed. Add the whipped topping; mix until well blended. Cut each cake layer horizontally in half, making a total of 4 cake layers. Place 1 cake layer cut side down on a platter and top with one quarter of the pumpkin mixture, spreading just to the edges. Repeat with the remaining layers of cake and pumpkin mixture 3 more times, ending with the pumpkin mixture and leaving the sides unfrosted. Cover loosely and chill for at least 3 hours before serving.

NOTE: Top with additional pecan halves for that fancy finishing touch.

No-Bake Holiday Fruitcake

18 to 20 servings

You know that old story about how most fruitcakes never get eaten, they're just passed on again as gifts? Well, that's not the case with this no-bake one. I mean, it's gonna get eaten . . . but sure, you can give it as a gift because it's one they're gonna really love!

1 package (16 ounces) graham crackers, crushed
2 containers (6 ounces each) candied cherries (1 each red and green), coarsely chopped
1 container (6 ounces) candied pineapple
2 cans (14 ounces each) sweetened condensed milk
1½ cups coarsely chopped pecans

Line a 9" × 5" loaf pan with plastic wrap, letting the wrap hang over the sides a few inches. In a large bowl, combine all the ingredients and thoroughly mix with your hands. Place the mixture in the lined pan and cover well. Freeze for at least 8 hours, or overnight, before serving. To serve, invert onto a serving platter, remove the pan and plastic wrap, and cut into slices. Store any remaining cake in the freezer.

NOTE: This is a very rich cake, so keep in mind that a small slice will go a long way!

Index

Index

Index

Index

Index

Index

Index

Mr. Food's Library Gives You More Ways to Say... "OOH IT'S SO GOOD!!"®

W I L L I A M   M O R R O W

A — Mr. Food Cooks Like Mama

B — THE MR. FOOD COOKBOOK — OOH it's so GOOD!!

C — MR. FOOD COOKS CHICKEN — "OOH IT'S SO GOOD!!"

D — MR. FOOD COOKS PASTA — "OOH IT'S SO GOOD!!"

E — MR. FOOD MAKES DESSERT

F — Mr. Food Cooks REAL AMERICAN — EASY, QUICK, FUN RECIPES — "OOH IT'S SO GOOD!!"

G — Mr. Food's FAVORITE COOKIES — EASY, QUICK, FUN RECIPES — "OOH IT'S SO GOOD!!"

H — Quick and Easy Side Dishes

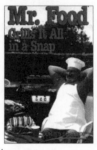

I — Mr. Food Grills It All in a Snap

J — Mr. Food's Fun Kitchen Tips and Shortcuts (and Recipes, Too!) — "OOH IT'S SO GOOD!!"

K — Old World Cooking Made Easy

L — "Help, Mr. Food! Company's Coming!"

M — Mr. Food Pizza 1-2-3

N — Mr. Food Meat Around the Table

O — MR. FOOD Simply CHOCOLATE

P — Mr. Food a little LIGHTER

Q — Mr. Food From My Kitchen to Yours: Stories and Recipes from Home

R — Mr. Food Easy Tex-Mex

S — Mr. Food One Pot, One Meal

T — Mr. Food COOL CRAVINGS

Mr. Food ®

Can Help You Be A Kitchen Hero!

Let Mr. Food® make your life easier with
Quick, No-Fuss Recipes and Helpful Kitchen Tips for

Family Dinners • Soups and Salads • Potluck Dishes • Barbecues • Special Brunches • Unbelievable Desserts

. . . and that's just the beginning!

Complete your Mr. Food® cookbook library today.
It's so simple to share in all the "OOH IT'S SO GOOD!!®"

✂ -

TITLE	PRICE	QUANTITY	
A. Mr. Food® Cooks Like Mama	@ $12.95 each	x _____	= $_____
B. The Mr. Food® Cookbook, OOH IT'S SO GOOD!!®	@ $12.95 each	x _____	= $_____
C. Mr. Food® Cooks Chicken	@ $ 9.95 each	x __/__	= $_____
D. Mr. Food® Cooks Pasta	@ $ 9.95 each	x _____	= $_____
E. Mr. Food® Makes Dessert	@ $ 9.95 each	x __/__	= $_____
F. Mr. Food® Cooks Real American	@ $14.95 each	x _____	= $_____
G. Mr. Food®'s Favorite Cookies	@ $11.95 each	x _____	= $_____
H. Mr. Food®'s Quick and Easy Side Dishes	@ $11.95 each	x _____	= $_____
I. Mr. Food® Grills It All in a Snap	@ $11.95 each	x _____	= $_____
J. Mr. Food®'s Fun Kitchen Tips and Shortcuts (and Recipes, Too!)	@ $11.95 each	x _____	= $_____
K. Mr. Food®'s Old World Cooking Made Easy	@ $14.95 each	x _____	= $_____
L. "Help, Mr. Food®! Company's Coming!"	@ $14.95 each	x _____	= $_____
M. Mr. Food® Pizza 1-2-3	@ $12.00 each	x _____	= $_____
N. Mr. Food® Meat Around the Table	@ $12.00 each	x _____	= $_____
O. Mr. Food® Simply Chocolate	@ $12.00 each	x __/__	= $_____
P. Mr. Food® A Little Lighter	@ $14.95 each	x _____	= $_____
Q. Mr. Food® From My Kitchen to Yours: Stories and Recipes from Home	@ $14.95 each	x _____	= $_____
R. Mr. Food® Easy Tex-Mex	@ $11.95 each	x _____	= $_____
S. Mr. Food® One Pot, One Meal	@ $11.95 each	x _____	= $_____
T. Mr. Food® Cool Cravings	@ $11.95 each	x _____	= $_____

Send payment to:
Mr. Food®
P.O. Box 9227
Coral Springs, FL 33075-9227

Name _____

Street _____ Apt._____

City _____ State_____ Zip_____

Method of Payment: ☐ Check or Money Order Enclosed

☐ Credit Card: ☐ Visa ☐ MasterCard Expiration Date _____

Signature _____

Book Total	$_____
+$2.95 Postage & Handling First Copy AND $1 Ea. Add'l. Copy (Canadian Orders Add Add'l. $2.00 Per Copy)	$_____
Subtotal	$_____
Less $1.00 per book if ordering 3 or more books with this order	$ – _____
Add Applicable Sales Tax (FL Residents Only)	$_____
Total in U.S. Funds	$_____

Account #: ☐ ☐ ☐ ☐ ☐ ☐ ☐ ☐ ☐ ☐ ☐ ☐ ☐ ☐ ☐ ☐ ☐

Please allow 4 to 6 weeks for delivery.

B